T

WE CELEBRATE

THE POWER
WE CELEBRATE

Women's Stories of Faith and Power

Edited by
Musimbi R.A. Kanyoro
and Wendy S. Robins

WCC Publications, Geneva

Cover design: Rob Lucas

ISBN: 2-8254-1038-1

© 1992 Lutheran World Federation,
150 route de Ferney, 1211 Geneva 2, Switzerland

Printed in Switzerland

Contents

Acknowledgments   vi

Foreword: The Beauty of Women's Revolt   vii
Mercy Amba Oduyoye

Introduction   1
Musimbi R. A. Kanyoro and Wendy S. Robins

EXPRESSIONS OF POWERLESSNESS

Of Gardens and Theology: Women of Faith Respond   5
Wanda Deifelt

The Power to Name   19
Musimbi R. A. Kanyoro

The Spider's Web of Triple Oppression   29
Jean Sindab

The Feminist Challenge   37
Ranjini Rebera

SCRIPTURE CAN EMPOWER WOMEN

Open Our Eyes   53
Raquel Rodríguez

The Dance of Liberation   62
Violet Cucciniello Little

Missing Persons   67
Constance F. Parvey

The Old, New Visions   73
Bärbel von Wartenberg-Potter

USING POWER

The Power to Communicate   83
Christa Berger

To Be a Servant Leader   90
Lynda Katsuno-Ishii

Practical Power   95
Wendy S. Robins

About the Authors   101

Acknowledgments

This book is a contribution of the Lutheran World Federation (LWF) to the Ecumenical Decade of Churches in Solidarity with Women.

Some of the material used in this book comes from meetings of Lutheran women and has been discussed by groups of women. These women have helped to shape the ideas in these chapters.

The LWF is particularly indebted to the women who took part in the International Consultation of Lutheran Women in Mexico City in 1989. Many of the contributions were presented for the first time at that gathering.

This book would not have been produced without the valuable and able assistance of Iris J. Benesch and Ana Villanueva, who were colleagues in the office of Women in Church and Society of the LWF. They have had the dual responsibility of being part of the organizing team of the consultation and preparing this manuscript through its various stages.

The staff of the Department of Studies, in which the office for Women in Church and Society was lodged, provided the inspiration for research leading to this publication.

Special thanks go to Wendy S. Robins, my co-editor, with whom working together has been a joy, a learning, and a growth. This is a second complete project on which we have worked jointly, the first being *Speaking for Ourselves* (WCC Publications, 1990).

Musimbi R. A. Kanyoro
Executive Secretary for Women in Church and Society

Foreword

The Beauty of Women's Revolt

This book is the product of a women's cooperative, the joint efforts of Christian women drawing on the life-enhancing resources of biblical and theological origins to speak out. They have been given voices by an inner conviction that they speak of the will of God for the human race and for all of creation. It is one more example of women's "gossip" whispered among women becoming a word for the ears of the whole community — a prophetic word of God's revolution against the misuse of power, and the announcement of good news that all the brothers too need to hear and to heed. Speaking out is central to this collection of essays. The beauty of the women's revolt against the silence imposed on women by culture, tradition, and religion is that women speak out of love for wholeness for themselves, after years of seeing only dirt, and wholeness for the whole creation too.

Women's experiences of life and interpretations of traditional myths are yet to become an integral part of human history. Women's reading of Scripture and theological reflections struggle for a place in the community of interpretation of the church. Hence the contemporary efforts to get women to write, to publish, to communicate, and to seek alternative communication avenues. Women's words are more often than not delivered as bold prints of real life — not just theories. Women speak of human beings as they struggle to keep their humanity under slum conditions, in the face of the brutalities of war and the anonymity imposed on women by the nonrecognition of their presence and contribution. Women call all to open their eyes to the realities of everyday life.

The beauty of women's revolt is that women listen to women; the culture of living to please men is over. Women listen to their inner power, the power of God calling them to respond as human beings who should relate directly to God. Women are significant because they are daughters of God, not because they are daughters of men. Women cry out, because they know God is close by and is listening and will act. Those who pick up sufficient courage to listen to women will hear stories not simply of victims but of resistance against the powers of evil. Women in this book tell stories of hope and challenge and of celebration of humanity released from bondage. Those who listen to women will hear them say: "It is necessary to set right the scales of divine justice, which have been distorted by human injustice" (Bärbel von Wartenberg-Potter). The struggle is to get men to tune their ears so they can hear women. Men who have come to realize the evils of patriarchy and women who know the shortcomings of matriarchy are called to listen together to what contemporary feminism has to offer in facing the challenges of human relations and ecological justice. Those men and women who open their ears to the words of "feminists" will hear a revolt against the ugliness of a world under the influence of evil impulses. These women, "born again" of the love of God and love for the fullness and wholeness of life, have refused to conform to this world and are calling all to be transformed by love so that they can become the bearers of love. The beauty of women's revolt is that it calls for the liberation of the enemy, which involves telling the truth in love and acting to make reconciliation possible.

In this collection we find the source of women's daring to challenge the accepted norms. Women reading the Bible for themselves have seen clearly that a life of oppression, enforced silenced, being battered into compliance with one's own and with others' dehumanization is in conflict with the world as God intended it. A crouching position is not the norm for human beings: we are meant to stand tall and to reach for the world beyond our human limitations, for it is God who brings in the new. Reaching out for the new has meant facing squarely what is familiar: searching for the meaning of power, understanding what it means for men and women to be sexual beings, challenging traditional understandings of the humanity of women.

The contributors to this collection are affirming the global nature of the quest. They are rooting themselves in the Christian tradition while conscious that there are other powerful influences at work in women's lives. They have attempted to move from a catalogue of women's woes to women's action for liberation. The collection gives a foretaste of the energy the human race will have occasion to celebrate and to appropriate when the daughters of faith are revealed in the fullness of their glory as daughters of God.

Mercy Amba Oduyoye

Introduction

Musimbi R. A. Kanyoro and Wendy S. Robins

When the World Council of Churches launched the Ecumenical Decade of Churches in Solidarity with Women, one of the objectives was said to be:

> Empowering women to challenge oppressive structures in the global community, their country and their church.

How can such empowerment take place? This book tries to provide some answers. For women to be empowered, their powerlessness must be identified and its roots must be analyzed. Thus, the first four articles in this book specifically address the circumstances of women's powerlessness. However, they go further and say that this situation needs to change, and women themselves must be part of the process of change. Women must take part in empowering themselves and in choosing the way of obtaining power in order to achieve the justice they seek.

We are people of the churches, the body of Christ, whose hope comes through the shared message of the Scriptures, and the book further shows that Scripture does empower individuals and societies. When Scripture is read with new eyes, the power of God's word becomes alive and new. It points to the new creation that was heralded by the coming of Jesus Christ. This new creation includes women. It seeks wholeness for those who are disadvantaged. The new creation does not take options for the mighty, but for the weak, the needy, the poor, the despised, the little ones, and the women.

Yet Scripture must be read with reflection and action. Theological *praxis* is important. Hence, another set of articles deals with the actions that may be taken. Some of these include becoming aware of the strength of mass media and how it shapes our thoughts and actions. Other ways involve being open to the alternatives suggested by women themselves after a thorough analysis of the social, economic, and political systems that diminish women. Analyzing the root causes includes analyzing the process of becoming power holders in a way that does not diminish others. So the book does not just end with blaming others, but addresses also the issues of women's use of power by themselves, for themselves, and among themselves.

The contributors to this volume come from varied geographical locations and cultures. Yet they all share a concern for being in solidarity with women. Whether the story of women is told from the Latin American, the Asian, the African, or the European setting, the plight and the pain of women still remain the same. Even affluent North America is not spared the need to empower women as full participants in the society.

This book is written for women and men who are willing to begin addressing this important issue of power sharing. As you use this book, ask yourself such questions as:

- Where are you in the power structure of your family, church, and society?

- How did you get there?

- Do you see power as a negative or positive attribute that you possess or lack?

- How do you share or distribute your power to others — or how do you attempt to get power if you have none?

- Does Scripture empower you or diminish you?

However you progress in this reflection, the materials in this book will help you to come to issues of the empowerment of women with new perspectives and ideas for action.

Expressions of
Powerlessness

Of Gardens and Theology: Women of Faith Respond

Wanda Deifelt

I would like to tell you a story. Once upon a time four women met and spoke and listened and touched. One was blind. One was deaf. One was mute. The fourth could see and hear and speak. This is their story. It is as true as you need it to be.

The blind woman spoke.

"Though I cannot see you, I sense that there are three women close to me. I have never asked this of anyone before, but do you think, would it be possible, if it's not too much trouble, could you listen to me and.... "

The woman who was mute began to sign for the woman who was deaf.

The blind woman continued.

"I have been told since birth that I cannot see, that I am blind. Though I do not know what 'seeing' means, I have listened. With my hands I have read and studied for many years and I am almost convinced that I, well, that I have visions. Please, I would not say these things to strangers except, well, I cannot stand them any longer. I 'see' — I'm sorry, there is no other word, I know it's inappropriate — I 'see' a world that is dying. The sun is often obscured by yellowish gray filth. The ground is mostly torn and trampled, where it is not suffocated under massive, heavy buildings. At night there are not enough stars visible to bother counting. Animals are crowded into pens, waiting to be slaughtered. There are men in this world, working in factories whose stacks spew poison into the air. These men are also being killed, though they do not seem to notice. There are women in this world, women who seem to be content to do what the dying men tell them. When they do not, they are scorned or beaten or ignored. This is what I 'see.' Please, what am I to do?"

The deaf woman spoke.

"With another's hands and my eyes I have 'heard' what you said. I do not find your story strange, for though I have been told since birth that I am deaf, I hear sounds in my head much of the time. This is what I 'hear.' Great crashings and clankings, deep moans and high, shrieking whistles. Low murmurs, sometimes oddly soothing. Harsh screams and dull, monotonous dronings. Occasionally chirps and hums. Cruel chortling, unexpected sobbing. These sounds have become too painful to bear."

Hesitantly, haltingly, the mute woman tried to speak.

"Some...times...like now, I...remember...having spoken... before. But when I did...I was told I couldn't speak. That is... how I...know I...cannot."

Finally, after a long silence, the fourth woman spoke.

"*I say you can*. Open your eyes, woman. Truly, you can see more clearly than those who told you that you were blind. Open your ears, woman. Truly, you can hear more clearly than those who told you that you were deaf. Open your mouth, woman. Truly, your words are needed now, far more than the words of those who told you that you cannot speak."

The fourth woman continued.

"As a child I was told that I was not a person. As a woman, I was told that I was not a real woman, because I did not dress as they told me to dress. Because I did not act as they told me to act. Because I did not see what they told me to see. Because I did not hear what they told me to hear. Because I did not say what they told me to say. This is my request. That you look at me. That you listen to me. That you speak to me."

And the women began to look and listen and speak and touch.[1]

Our Stories as Theology

A long journey has brought us this far, a journey of faith that connects us to one another and affirms our need to hear each other's stories. All are members of a global community. All are part of a web of life and death that surrounds each one in different ways. Women need each other's support for their struggles. We need sisters to listen to our pain, to share our hopes, to tell us that there are dreams to be dreamed and realities to be changed, and that we can do it.

We need to look and listen and speak and touch. We encounter each other as women of faith with faith in ourselves and faith in each other. Each one of us has a wealth of experiences to share. We need to affirm each other's gifts, to affirm each other as full human beings, created in the image of God. We believe that our sisters have something to say and we should listen to it. We need to listen to each other's struggles. We have been growing and look forward to growing further in our understanding of ourselves as women who have a task: to make this a better world.

For many, talking and listening to each other is like arriving at an oasis, with fresh water and shady palm trees, after a long journey in the wilderness. It is a chance to be refreshed after the tiresome journey, to pull down our hair and take off our sweaty sandals. It has been a long journey, but we are not alone. As we sit down to rest, we tell our sisters of the things that have gone before. We tell of the struggle to survive. We talk of hunger, diseases; of never-ending work; lovers, children, and friends. We talk about oppression, exploitation of labor and sexual harassment. We also talk about visions of a better world, of equality, and of liberation. When we feel renewed in our energies and hopes, we will move on into the desert again. We have a chance to look, to listen, to speak, to touch, and we will do the same after our departure from the oasis.

As women we often come together to share our stories, to tell our hopes for our church, to support each other's ministries and our calls to discipleship. But when we tell our stories and our visions, they are never just our own. When I tell about my life, I am telling about the lives of my sisters, my mother and grandmothers, about the women who have somehow shaped me. I feel free to invoke their presence, even though they are not there physically. I want to tell my story as a statement of faith that women's stories *must* be told. With this telling, with this sharing, women begin to connect with each other as women, honestly and with integrity. This is my way of telling the stories of the women in my life whose stories would otherwise be forgotten — forgotten because no one would deem their lives important enough to write them down. These are everyday stories, of kitchens and fields and factories. My story is their story, and it is a story of pain and joy.

A Story of Gardens and Theology

I am a Brazilian woman living in Chicago, doing Ph.D. work in feminist theology. The unusual thing about me is that I have a garden where I live, and when I garden the world stops to chat. I live in an apartment building, and for three years I have had my eyes on the abandoned courtyard of our building. I got tired of seeing only weeds growing and finally borrowed a shovel from one friend and a hoe from another and got the garden going. My husband thinks that it is just another excuse for me to run away from my desk. I should be writing my Ph.D. dissertation, and here I am, gardening instead. But I know better, for I get more out of an hour of gardening than I do from a whole day reading Bultmann or Barth or anybody else. Indeed, I do theology while I'm pulling weeds and planting flowers. I feel connected to struggles for justice when my friend from South Africa stops to introduce me to another South African. They tell me about their families who are still back home, and how they fear for their lives. Things will get worse before they get better, they say. I feel peace when my Korean friend passes by and nods approvingly while my Malaysian friend and her children entertain themselves in the garden.

I live in an unusual place, for there is a little part of the world represented in every corner of our building. Last week I was digging a hole to plant some lilies, and my neighbor from Burma stopped and asked whether she could work a little bit. Of course, I said. She started shoveling and talking: "You know, this reminds me so much of home," she said. "It brings back childhood memories: my mom and I digging the rice fields back in Burma, my father turning the muddy soil with his buffalo...." So we started talking about how similar, and how different, are my home country and Burma. I too remembered my grandfather working the land in southern Brazil and the red earth sticking to the plough as he turned the soil.

My Mother's Garden

Talking with my friends brought back memories of that first garden, where my mother grew her vegetables and her roses, her herbs and spices. Those were the days of my innocence, my garden of Eden, when I didn't know there could be any troubles. News of military coups, nuclear war, and the torture of thousands of men and women could not reach me in that protected environment. My mother and I spent long hours working in the garden. Most of the time she didn't speak much because she thought what she had to say was not important. So we had long silences together instead of long talks together. Instead of talking, she developed a special talent for listening to people. There were always women coming over to visit her. These women came to talk about their husbands, their children, their diseases. They needed somebody to listen, and my mother was there.

My mother, like most women I know, does not think that her work is important. In the First World she would probably be called a counsellor or a psychologist if she had the proper training. Instead, she sees her gift of listening as just another thing women do. She has no leadership role whatsoever in the church or in her community. If anybody would even suggest such a thing, saying that she has gifts and talents, she would laugh. She keeps telling herself how little she knows, that she is not capable, that others can do it better. She works hard to diminish herself. She has been brought up believing that her opinions don't count.

I realized later that my mother was not the only one who continuously belittled herself. Women in general are educated to believe that being born female means to be born innately inferior, damaged, that there is something wrong with us. We are told that we are needed as mothers, caretakers, cheap labor in the fields and factories. We are told that we are also needed in our church, to do the fund raising and the cleaning. We are told every day that the world needs our bodies and our work. We are told that without us the church would not exist. We are not given an equal place because we live in a society that is based on the existence of "others." These "others" are women, blacks, native populations, disabled people, gay men and lesbian women, the poor.

I am afraid that the church is not better off. In many places around the world, being a woman still means that you have to stay on the other side of the pulpit: silenced, not ordained. Being a woman means to do the hard work and have little say in the process of decision making. As Bell Hooks explains:

> Women are the group most victimized by sexist oppression. As with other forms of group oppression, sexism is perpetuated by institutional and social structures; by the individuals who dominate, exploit or oppress; and by the victims themselves who are socialized to behave in ways that make them act in complicity with the status quo.[2]

I am aware that sometimes it is easier to portray ourselves only as "victims." I think it is necessary to recognize that women are co-opted into this system and are tempted to live up to the expectations that society has for them, which are small. It is easier and more secure to hold on to the traditional ways, such as women doing most of the work in the church and men having most of the leadership. Many women still believe that this is the only way of being church or are afraid of taking more prominent roles in church and society. But women are not just victims of this game, and there is a great danger in perceiving ourselves only as such. As Beverly Harrison says,

> The deepest danger to our cause is that our anger will turn inward and lead us to portray ourselves and other women chiefly as victims rather than those who have struggled for the gift of life against incredible odds. The creative power of anger is shaped by owning this great strength of women and others who have struggled for the full gift of life against structures of oppression.[3]

A Garden with Friends

I grew up, moved away from home when I was fourteen, and entered seminary when I was seventeen. There I ate the apple of knowledge and found out about the existence of good and evil. Having left the garden of Eden, which was my mother's garden, I was faced with the need to till the ground on my own. I discovered that there was injustice in the world, that there was much poverty. I realized that my family was not the only one going through hardships because of the Brazilian economy. More than 75 percent of all Brazilians are deprived in one way or another of those things that are considered fundamental to normal life: food, clothing, health care, education. My family was still better off than most, but I started seeing that changes were necessary at political and economic levels to improve the life conditions of all people.

My next recollection is of myself and five other women dragging dozens of buckets full of soil to start a garden in our backyard. While we worked, we also talked about ourselves, our hopes and fears, and of what it meant to be a woman pastor in the Lutheran Church. If those five women had not been there, I might not have finished my studies at the seminary. During the first months I had biblical passages quoted at me every day by some fundamentalist students, telling me that I should be quiet in church, that as a woman I had no right to study theology, and that I should find myself a husband and go home to be a good Christian housewife instead.

While we were gardening we also talked about the limited opportunities open to our mothers and grandmothers. My mother's story wasn't very different from other women's stories. She wanted so much to study when she was growing up. But there was only one elementary school in the village, and she would have had to go to the city if she wanted to continue studying. That meant she would have had to stay with a relative and work for room and board, as well as attending school. My grandfather was opposed to the idea. Why waste time and money on her education if she was going to get married and have children anyway? Better that she stay home. My friends and I grieved for what our mothers could have been. We grieved for what they never became. How much my mother longed for knowledge and how passionately she spoke when she told my sister and me that no sacrifice would be too much if only we got a good education. While talking with my friends I came to realize that her story of self-sacrifice was not an exception as I thought, but the rule.

At that time I started to suspect that traditional theology did not take the lives of women such as my mother and grandmothers into account. I kept reading that sin, for example, was pride and the will-to-power. But I did not see that in their lives. Did it mean that they were saints? I found out only later that maybe sin as pride and the will-to-power is a male problem. Perhaps women's sin is the opposite: that we have too little will-to-power. I firmly believe that my mother's self-sacrifice is an example of systemic sin. I also believe that the discrimination women suffer, the frequent exclusion from decision making, and regarding women as second-class citizens are evils and not at all the will of God. Maybe women's sin is self-denial, the dependence on others for self-affirmation, and the lack of confidence in our capabilities.[4] It is very sad that all these traits are still perceived as virtues by the church.

The Peruvian theologian Gustavo Gutiérrez says that any social system that denies the full humanity of people, that prevents human beings from attaining life in abundance, and that keeps millions of human beings living in oppression and exploitation is sinful.[5] I believe that women in Latin America, especially poor women, lesbian women, disabled women, and women of color are among the most oppressed human beings. Yet their experiences are not taken into account because in many cases women's lives are not seen as being worth much. To illustrate this, I move to my next garden and my next story.

Of Gardening and Childbearing

In 1982, I was working with Bishop Pedro Casaldáliga for a couple of months in one of the rural base communities in the Amazon area. In the back of the little shack in which we lived we had a little garden. Every day we dragged buckets of water from the stream

nearby to irrigate the spinach crop. There was, of course, no elec-
tricity, no water apart from the stream, and our shack was very poor.
We really relied on the stream. Every day the French priest and the
Brazilian nun (two of the members of the group with which I was
working) had an argument about whether the best time to water the
spinach was early in the morning or late afternoon. I don't know
who defended which position, but we were having this discussion
one afternoon when one of our neighbors came with the news that
Maria had come to town to deliver her baby and to ask if one of us
could come over and help. Perhaps because I wasn't too interested
in the "watering the spinach symposium," I volunteered to go, after
I was assured that the doctor was already there.

Maria was only thirty-two years old, and this was her eighth pregnancy. She had had three miscarriages, and the doctor had advised
her not to have another baby. But because she suffered from mal-
nutrition, the birth control pills the doctor had given her (which
Maria had hidden from her husband) didn't work. So she was pregnant again. Also she was very weak. After spending hours in labor,
she finally delivered a baby girl. But Maria was not recovering. She
was bleeding too much. I had never before seen death and life so
closely linked. The baby girl was screaming "life," and Maria, who
had brought forth life, who had given life, was dying. What a con-
tradiction. I thought of the reality that surrounded us: powerful
landowners hiring thugs to get rid of the leaders of the base community, including the nun, the priest, and even, perhaps, me because we
were vocally denouncing their illegal appropriation of public land.
But the fear of my own death, through these thugs, seemed very
unreal as I watched Maria bleed away. She was dying because of the
hemorrhage.

Only by chance did the doctor have the proper medicine to stop
the bleeding. She kept trying to find a vein in Maria's arm, poking
her several times without success. Finally, she found the vein. As
the medicine was taking effect, we looked at each other, not quite
believing the miracle that had just taken place. Not the miracle of a
baby, but the miracle that Maria was alive. She had survived. Then
the doctor told her that another pregnancy would be fatal, that she
would most certainly die. She also told Maria that there were ways
to prevent her from having another baby, perhaps a tubal ligation.
Maria didn't have the financial means for that, but the doctor assured
her that the community health center would help. Maria, still very
weak, turned her head toward the wall to avoid looking the doctor in

her eyes and said that it was not up to her to decide. The doctor had to ask her husband. The doctor walked out of the room, called the husband aside, and explained what needed to be done. The husband, however, wouldn't allow the operation: "What would my friends say if I didn't have any more children." He was, in effect, asking what would happen to his male pride.

I don't know what happened to Maria. I never heard of her again. But I know that once in the Amazon area I helped to deliver a baby, and doing this opened my eyes. Maria is one of the women who have shaped my life. She was my conversion to feminism. From my mother I learned that women don't own their minds. From Maria I learned that women don't own their bodies. It was wrong. It was unfair. This should be different. A new consciousness was born in me, that women have the right to give birth to themselves, that women can make decisions regarding their bodies, that women are human beings.

Maria's story might be shocking to First World women, but women who live in Third World countries know that Maria's story repeats itself every day. It is not only the threat of dying in labor. Violence at home, rape, and prostitution are just a few among the many abuses suffered by women. For me, the most shocking symptoms of the diseased society we live in are the children, nine to twelve years old, pushed into prostitution because of the poverty in which they live.[6] Children are selling their bodies for a piece of bread. This is dehumanizing and we need to stop it. We need to name this situation as oppressive, and we need to work for radical changes.

A Garden Pointing toward Reconciliation

When I talk about women's oppression in Brazil, I also have to talk about the struggles of women to achieve full humanity. In most cases, all their energy goes into the struggle to be alive one more day. But there are cases of people who go beyond this. I am reminded of the collective garden we had in Belem do Para, in northern Brazil, when I was working with Marga, one of the few female Lutheran pastors of our church in Brazil. The plot of land behind the house had once been a car repair shop with a junkyard attached to it. Every day Marga and I worked in the garden, clearing it out. In the beginning there was only Marga and me, so the process was very slow. Then the children in the neighborhood became interested in the project as well, and they started coming over after school. Then a couple of teenagers joined in. Meanwhile, we already had a little crop going, along with several banana, papaya, and mango trees.

One Sunday we had a large group over for a short retreat on popular journalism. We were to show how people without many resources could put out their own newsletter and pamphlets by improvising with a homemade printer. For me, however, the highlight of the day was the lunch we had with vegetables and fruits from the garden. I kept thinking of Micah's vision of turning swords into ploughshares and spears into pruning hooks (Mic. 4:3) and how closely related that was to turning a junkyard into a garden. This was a very special garden. It was not a garden in which only one individual ate the fruit of everybody else's labor, but where people worked together and fed themselves from their work. Even better, they also had plenty to share with others. The work in the garden was connected to the art of writing pamphlets and community newsletters. We were getting people together to work and to make a difference in their environment.

This garden became a symbol of a community for me, of white and black, old and young, male and female, working together, side by side. In my mind, places like this one, where people are struggling for life, are gardens where seeds of the Reign of God can be found. They are like fingers pointing to the possibility of reconciliation. Reconciliation here is not only a bringing together of otherwise opposite parties, overlooking the conflicts. To the contrary. I am aware that throughout history the idea of reconciliation has been used to make content and submissive those who are unsatisfied. How many times have oppressed groups been denied the right to protest and to speak up for themselves in the name of unity and the common good? What was happening in Belem and what is happening in other Christian base communities, neighborhood associations, labor unions, and Bible study groups is a commitment to improve the situation of the people involved in them, to work hard to make this a better world. It is a commitment to improve the situation of the people, to denounce injustice, and to bring about signs that changes are possible. It is a commitment to choose life instead of death.

So far, the community garden in Belem has been the closest I have been to a holistic work experience. It was hard work and pleasure at the same time. It was working the soil and working with human beings. It was growing vegetables and feeding hungry people. It was a chance to take care of myself and to take care of others.

It was the embodiment of working together, whether I worked in the garden or taught people to read and write in their literacy program. What was important for me was the feeling of being connected to the struggles of other people and that, wherever I worked, I was making a difference.

Of Gardens and Theology

My mother's garden, the garden of my women friends at the seminary, the garden in the Amazon area, the community garden in Belem, and the garden I work now in Chicago have become symbols for my own theological work. Theology and gardens are closely related because I can do neither of them in isolation. My work can be effective only if I am connected to other people, if I can relate what I am doing to their lives and struggles. Marta Benavides said something about gardening that inspired me to connect gardens to theology:

> It is important for me to garden with others. To garden with others is an expression of solidarity; that is what being *compañeras* is all about. Gardening is visioning, dreaming, and futuring for me too. It is to envision and bring about the new earth, right here and now. But I cannot bring about the new earth by myself, because a new earth demands that we look at the universe in which we are immersed. We must see what is old and decadent and death-giving: infant mortality, unemployment, profit valued more than people, militarism, the arms race. We must look for the new we are called to bring forth: health and education for everyone, soil conservation, food with no preservatives or pesticides.[7]

Planting gardens and doing theology show my desire for roots, for grounding and connection. They reflect my desire to build community, to make a difference. Gardening and theology are about visions and hopes and hard work. They are also about patience and faith and care. Sometimes, when we pull the weeds of oppression and plant the seeds of justice, our gardens get trampled by those who disagree with us. The lives of many women and men are cut short because of this. To have a garden trampled sometimes means that women are not allowed to live up to their full potential, but other times it means actual death. Margarida Alves was a union leader in Northeast Brazil, and she was killed by the thugs of a powerful landowner in the area. Margarida was working to organize small farmers, men and women, trying to persuade them not to give in to the landowner's threats. Margarida, in Portuguese, means daisy, a flower. She was trampled by the boots of a powerful landowner. But instead of dismantling the union, the small farmers continued their struggle, saying that from Margarida's blood a new people and a new society would be born. I say: Margarida, from your seeds a new garden will be planted.

Each of us has been called to live out the gifts we have received and to do that in the context in which we are located. We are called to work and struggle. We are asked to respond and take action. We are invited to participate actively in a global community that needs our involvement. We are led to look into situations of oppression and exploitation, situations of death and misery. We must respond.

In a garden everything is in balance and has a purpose. The purpose of one plant is not to live in isolation, but together with other plants to make a beautiful, colorful, and plentiful garden. When you bring together different plants in a garden, you end up with a rich variety of colors, sizes, and shapes. Each of us is also part of a community that brings together the experiences and memories of people that are part of it. Each of us is connected to this community, to this garden, and in it we all play equally important roles.

When you plant flowers side by side, you have to make sure that each one has enough space. As women, we have to make sure that each one of us has space, that we are not strangled by the weeds of discrimination. Each of us has to have the freedom to say what we think and believe, knowing that it is also necessary to listen to each other. This means that we have to affirm equality among ourselves, even though society and church don't always act in this way.

In a flower bed, sometimes you plant flowers of different colors side by side. Variety of colors makes a garden beautiful: a red flower becomes brighter when it is next to a white or a yellow one. What it means here is that we too come in different colors, that we speak different languages, that we have different cultures. We are not asked to give up our identity in order to meet as women. We have to acknowledge our differences and our particular stories if we want to talk as equals. In this garden, each woman keeps her identity and is encouraged to live up to her full potential.

Each plant needs enough light and water to survive. What I see happening is that some corners of our global garden have appropriated a large amount of resources, depriving most of the plants of the necessary nutrients. You know what happens when a few plants get all the fertilizer and water while the rest get nothing at all. The plants that are overfed become too big to handle, and, if they are vegetables, they become stale and taste like straw. The plants that are underfed don't grow. They shrink and die. In our global garden, the majority of the people who live in the Third World live in subhuman conditions. They are the Marias, the Margaridas, and the ten-year-old children who work as prostitutes. We are called to do work of solidarity. We must listen, look, speak, and touch. We do that in the spirit of sisterhood, as women who feel connected to each other in our struggles for life. We must affirm our gifts and talk about new ways of exercising those gifts. We must share our visions. We need to support each other's ministries because each of us has been called forth to make a difference in the world. We already do work of passion and compassion; now is the time to affirm our work as legitimate and necessary. We must tell our stories. We must claim our garden.

Notes

1. Lucy Tatman, "For Women," unpublished manuscript, 1989.
2. Bell Hooks, *Feminist Theory: From Margin to Center* (Boston: South End, 1984), 43.
3. Beverly Wildung Harrison, *Making the Connections: Essays in Feminist Social Ethics* (Boston: Beacon Press, 1985), 7.
4. Judith Plaskow, *Sex, Sin and Grace* (Lanham, Md.: University Press of America, 1980), 170.
5. Gustavo Gutiérrez, *A Theology of Liberation: History, Politics and Salvation* (Maryknoll, N.Y.: Orbis Books, 1973), 295.
6. Carolina Carlessi, "Region's Women Confront Deep-rooted Sexual Abuse," *Latinamerica Press* (February 27, 1986): 3–4.
7. Marta Benavides, "My Mother's Garden Is a New Creation," in *Inheriting Our Mother's Garden: Feminist Theology in Third World Perspective*, ed. Letty M. Russell and others (Philadelphia: Westminster Press, 1988), 133–34.

Bibliography

Benavides, Marta. "My Mother's Garden Is a New Creation." In *Inheriting Our Mother's Gardens: Feminist Theology in the Third World Perspective*, ed. Letty M. Russell and others, Philadelphia: Westminster Press, 1988.
Boff, Leonardo. *Igreja: Carisma y poder: Ensaios de eclesiología militante*. Petrópolis: Vozes, 1980; Eng. trans.: *Church: Charism and Power*. New York: Crossroad, 1985.
Hooks, Bell. *Feminist Theory: From Margin to Center*. Boston: South End Press, 1984.
Carlessi, Carolina. "Region's Women Confront Deep-rooted Sexual Abuse." *Latinamerica Press*, February 27, 1986.
Fiorenza, Elisabeth Schüssler. *In Memory of Her: A Feminist Theological Reconstruction of Christian Origins*. New York: Crossroad, 1984.
Gebara, Ivone, and Maria Clara Bingemer. *Maria, Mãe de Deus e Mãe dos Pobres: Um Ensaio a partir da Mulher e da America Latina*. Petrópolis: Vozes, 1987; Eng. trans.: *Mary, Mother of God, Mother of the Poor*. Maryknoll, N.Y.: Orbis Books, 1989.
Gutiérrez, Gustavo. *A Theology of Liberation: History, Politics and Salvation*. Maryknoll, N.Y.: Orbis Books, 1973.

Harrison, Beverly Wildung. *Making the Connection: Essays in Feminist Social Ethics.* Boston: Beacon Press, 1985.

Mesters, Carlos. *Por tras das palavras: Um Estudo sobre a porta de entrada no mundo da Biblia.* Petrópolis: Vozes, 1980.

Plaskow, Judith. *Sex, Sin and Grace: Women's Experience and the Theologies of Reinhold Niebuhr and Paul Tillich.* Lanham, Md.: University Press of America, 1980.

The Power to Name

Musimbi R. A. Kanyoro

The following are true stories of church women in Africa. The names and their churches are disguised.

I sat with the group of thirty women on the benches of the church to which I had been invited. None of the women spoke. The two men did all the talking. They told me how women are disorganized and lack education, professions, and ambition. "We try hard to assist these women to wake up and do something for the church, but we find no response. They are lazy. They find it difficult to be on time for the meetings we call. They do not have any ideas. We have asked them to come up with plans of action for their program, but received no response."

For three hours I thought, Why can't a sister say something to me? Then after three hours, the busy men had to leave the meeting to go to pay attention to more pressing church matters. The women stayed.

For three minutes, silence continued. Fear suddenly grabbed me. How would I handle this silence? The silence was so loud that it hurt my ears. I wanted to hear someone talk. Anything would have soothed my aching ears.

I looked hard into the faces of thirty women. My interpreter began to assume the position of the departed men. She felt my discomfort and started to probe. "Let us tell our sister about our problems. We have no money..." she began. No sooner had she opened her mouth than the tall, elegant-looking woman wearing a clean old red dress, the one whose name I was to learn, motioned her to stop. Agnes took the floor. Agnes listened to the fading steps of the departing men. Then Agnes spoke. "You do not invite a guest to tell her that you have no food," she said. "Our sister has come to visit us. We want her to visit us. We want her to know us. We want her to know our houses, our children, our

19

husbands. We want her to see what we do, how we live, eat, sleep, and worship."

In this way the meeting broke up. I had four days to visit the church. The church had already decided that the women did not have much to offer to an executive from headquarters, and so they had arranged visits and discussions with important people. But Agnes just took over. In a few minutes, the women made their arrangements. Then they smiled and bid me goodbye, saying we would soon see each other.

Taking Care of Each Other

I went with Agnes's group. First we took a bus for two hours. Then we walked. She said it was quite near. When my feet complained, the clock confirmed that the brisk walking had lasted for two hours. The hot African sun did not make the journey feel shorter.

When we got to her home, the women were waiting. How did they know? Who were they? They welcomed us with song. Soon we were eating. The women talked. They talked about everything. Zipporah told of how as a young girl she was married off to a young evangelist. The church had been afraid that the evangelist would fall into temptation, so they looked around for a Sunday School teacher to marry him. Zipporah had to leave school. Since then, her life has been in the village, digging and tilling the land. The evangelist went away to study. He read many books. He became very clever and big. To him, Zipporah became very small and stupid. She became narrow-minded and dirty. The evangelist fell into temptation. He left the church. Every time Zipporah sees him come home to the village with his new educated, wife Zipporah cries.

The women listened to Zipporah. They laughed as if the story were funny. She laughed with them. They teased her: "Zipp! What would we have done without you? You work hardest among us. You are our leader."

Yes, the Sunday School teacher became the leader. She could read and write. Bilha took over and told me about their group.

There are about two hundred women in five villages. "We were bored of always being in the same village. We wanted friends. We wanted to go somewhere and do something different. It all began in our village in church one Sunday. Zipporah got us together. We wanted to begin a women's group where we could take care of one another." I had to interrupt and ask for the exact words to be repeated. Yes — "Take care of one another."

So we formed this group, and on Sundays after church we would see who was not in church and send someone to see if there was sickness in the home. The rest of us would assemble in one of our homes and sing and pray and talk.

Then Damaris jumped in! "It is always a great delight when you know that the girls will be coming to your house. You sweep the house, you prepare something nice to eat, you even persuade your man to let you slaughter some chickens." They laughed again· in agreement with Damaris.

"Yes," the chorus roared and the conversation went on. "As we visited each other, we started to learn about ourselves. Some people had much food, others struggled, but everyone was surviving. In some homes we sat on the chairs, and in others just on the floor because there were no chairs. Some of us started to feel embarrassed as we got to see how others lived. In fact, a few of us dropped out because we talked to our husbands about what we had seen, and we were forbidden to meet with other women again."

Lois, the one who seemed the quietest, jumped in. "I was one of those who dropped out. My husband said I must not compare our lives to other people's." Then Beliza added, "I dropped out because I told my husband not to beat me any longer, after I found out that some men don't beat their wives. Before I became part of the group, I always assumed that it was a husband's right to beat his wife. I had seen my father beat my mother. My brother also beats his wife."

Bilha picked up the story again and told it quickly.

"We wanted to take care of each other, but we found that our meetings were dividing and hurting us. So we stopped moving from home to home and decided to meet in the church, after the service. We asked ourselves how we could help each other. We soon came up with so many suggestions that it was difficult to decide what to do. In the end we decided to help each other by working as teams on our farms. We wanted to learn new ways to farm. So we asked our husbands to get us somebody to teach us how to use fertilizer. Then we made a duty rota. All of us would go to one person's farm, work on it very hard, and finish it. We would then move to the next person's. Work became very interesting and easy for us. We could take our children with us, and one of us would mind all the children while the rest worked. If one of the mothers needed to stop and breast feed her baby, the rest of the group just dug her part. We were so busy and so happy that other women heard of our group and joined. When we became too large, we broke up into smaller groups according to where we lived.

"During the third year, we found that our crops had very good yields. Even the men were happy, and they stopped hindering us from joining groups.

"Then we began to do other things besides farming. We thought it a good idea for every woman to have an iron-roofed house so that, if her husband is away, she does not have to cope with rain!"

I stopped them to ask what they meant by this. Zipporah joined in to explain. "By our customs, women do not thatch houses. That is a man's duty. If a man has lots of wives and does not like some, he just refuses to repair the roofs of the houses belonging to the wives who have fallen out of favor. He may also refuse to repair the roof of an only wife to punish her for some reason or other. But in most cases, men move out to work in the cities. They earn very little money and can only come home once in six months. Then it is very hard on the wife and children if the rains come and the house leaks."

This explanation told it all. So I listened again. Bilha continued to explain to me how each group contributes money for materials for the houses. Then they offer their labor for all work except thatching the roof. I could see many iron-roofed houses. The women had built them.

Then Agnes came back to the scene. She had been sitting contributing a word or so, but mostly concentrating on braiding the hair of her school-going teenager. The girl's hair was now completed with corn-rows all over her head. I observed her and wondered what she would be in two decades' time.

Agnes commanded that we move on. The second group was waiting. Half an hour later, we were at a completely different village. I could even see a change in the crops and definitely in the names and the language. Rabei, the leader of the new group, was a shy young woman. "I am a parish worker," Rabei told me as she began to show me work done by women in her parish. She took me to a big store full of crafts of all shapes and sizes. "We are waiting for the mission vehicle that comes once in three months to collect these baskets for sale."

I was curious and asked what they do with the money they get. "We never see it. The missionary gives it to the church. It is money for God. It does God's work."

Looking at Rabei's aging clothes, bare feet, and the smile on her face, I felt like I was in the presence of God's angel — a servant of God standing there right with me, together with her group of angels.

Then Doris, the one trained in social work, wanted to demonstrate her skills. I watched as her quick hands moved from left to right, left to right, and then center, to keep the central threads of reed firm and straight. I grieved in my heart. Here they are, named as unskilled, unschooled, unemployed women. They are denied the power to name themselves. Then I turned and looked directly into Doris's face. She laughed, and invited me to try her skill. I tried. I failed. We all laughed and went outside to celebrate. The group sang, danced, beat the drums. Yes, we celebrated. Agnes had expressed it correctly, "Come and see us." I had come and seen them.

Other People's Meetings

I got back to the city in the late hours of the evening. The sun was beginning to go down. The four walls of the modern guest house imprisoned me. I tried to jot down some notes and found myself confused, unskilled. I cried myself to sleep. I woke up to get ready for the board meeting. Agnes was coming too. I wondered who else would come. The pastor had said that women leaders would be there to welcome me to this special meeting.

The meeting began. The men talked. Agnes said nothing. The women kept silent. They were criticized; they were ignored; they were challenged. I looked in their faces and smiled silently. I listened hard to the talking men and heard nothing. The meeting finished. I left the city and went with Agnes. For three days we walked, we talked, we sang, and we worked. Then Agnes named it. She said it to me. I still hear her say it. Listen to it. Hear it with me:

"The meetings in the church are not our meetings. They want us women to talk, but they do not listen. Our words are useless. What we do is good only for women. Can they not see what we are doing? Can they not see that we women pay school fees for the children through our sweat? Can they not see the houses? Can they not see that every woman has friends who visit her when she is sick and help her with her work? Can they not see the church in our lives?"

I listened to this woman, this eloquent woman with self-pride. Is it true? Is silence power too? Is this woman who has never gone to school telling me that we cannot merely react to the questions posed by patriarchy? Is she telling me that we need the power to move our own issues?

Many days after we had parted, I still heard Agnes. I still hear her today. I hear her tell me that we women must be able to ask our own questions and we need space to do that. I hear her tell me that we must not break our silence where our talk is not valued, for that is equivalent to throwing pearls to swine. But I also hear her tell me that when we talk of women and the church, or women and theology, we must not expect women just to turn up and have a ride in an already moving vehicle. Women must be part of the decision to choose the vehicle in which to move.

But even as I hear Agnes talk to me, I am still puzzled that her determination does not get her very far in matters concerning her views on life and the church. Africa is full of women like Agnes, determined women, who have decided to take seriously the saying that "actions speak louder than words." But these actions still go unnoticed in their families, their churches, and society. Women continue to raise funds for church use, including subsidies for pastors' salaries. They continue to build community centers for the church out of their own meager income. Their little offering, equivalent to the widow's mite, is still the most important local income of the churches. African women support their families and society in food production and in the nurturing and education of the children. But how and when will African churches and society open doors for women to share and use their will power for the benefit of the whole church? How and when will African women celebrate the sharing of power in leadership positions of church and society? How and when will women be given their due respect in the structure of the family?

Today many African women have begun to question the silence they have so preciously guarded for decades. African women theologians meeting in Accra in September 1989 urged each other to arise and break the silence. They understood the Scriptures to be challenging the image of an African woman, known to church and society only through her services. By examining various Scriptures, the African theologians found out that Jesus' encounter with women was always followed by a command that involved speech. To the bleeding woman (Luke 8:40–48) Jesus demanded that she tell her story after being healed. The Samaritan woman had to brave a debate with Jesus (John 4:1–26). Are these Scriptures not challenging African women to combine their actions with words, words of complaint and even of debate with the authorities?

The command that the risen Christ gave to the women was to go and tell the disciples that the Savior is risen. Thus, women are commanded to speak out and tell the good news. To be able to tell the good news, women need a new platform. They need a new audience. They need new rules and regulations through which their words and deeds will be seen and known. Women need new power. They need to belong to new decision-making structures where they can contribute and be valued for their gifts. The gifts and activities of women must get recognition and become part of the church's "God-talk." Without these possibilities, women remain outside the power circle of church and society. Their activities remain outside the recorded chronicles of the church, for it is only those with power that have a voice to shape and determine history. His-story it will remain, and never will her-story be told until she is willing to become a power broker too. However, women should not try to be power brokers in structures and institutions that are already diseased.

Positions without Power

There are a few women in leadership positions in the churches in Africa. Who are they? How do they use their woman power in these new positions within the existing structures?

Joyce, a member of the Executive Committee, came to meet me at the airport. Her attire and the car she drove were clear indications that she was not a full-time employee of the church. As we began talking, I soon learned that she was a daughter of the former bishop. She had obtained a church scholarship to study abroad, and on her return, she had gotten a good job with an international organization. Joyce is knowledgeable about many things. She is kind and active in the church. But her life has always been "separate," one of isolation. As a daughter of the bishop, she grew up in a big house that had been built by, and for, missionaries. Both her parents were educated. Her mother worked as a nurse until her husband became a bishop. Then she left her job to devote time to attending to church visitors.

Joyce does not see her position on the Executive Committee as having anything to do with being a woman. She is qualified for the job and has historical family links with the church. Joyce contributes to all debates and decisions of the church, but she is content, like her other colleagues, with the agenda as it is. Joyce does not even notice the absence of women on the agenda. She does not even notice that she is the only woman on the Executive Committee. In committee meetings, Joyce is always asked to perform all the secretarial tasks. When there are guests coming to the church, she is asked to draw up the hosting activities. Joyce has grown up seeing her mother participate in this way, and therefore there is no other model of women's participation in her system.

Elizabeth is the director for women's work in her church. That position entitles her to attend board meetings. However, she does not have a voting right. According to tradition, the women's leader comes to the meetings to give a report on her work when, and if, she is asked. Otherwise, she is not expected to say anything. In relating her story, Elizabeth said she was not happy with this arrangement. She thinks her self-worth and that of the women she leads is not taken seriously. She also feels marginalized, pushed to the side. She does not contribute to the welfare of the whole church. Elizabeth sees her membership of the board as being completely powerless. Elizabeth has never made a difference to the board meetings.

Deborah was employed as a deputy staff executive. As soon as she began the job, new job assignments were made. The chief executive said that Deborah could not do the job of a deputy because it involved working late outside office hours, much travel, and meetings with important church men. All these things were not good for a married woman. Deborah has small children still going to school. Her husband is a director of a big company and is often away on business trips or has late appointments. Deborah is familiar with what the life of an executive can be like. When she was first appointed, she thought church executive jobs would be different. When her boss told her that it was no different, Deborah was content for all her powers to be removed. She is now in charge of church properties and staff disputes. Deborah does not attend any of the important meetings even when they are at the church headquarters. She still keeps the title of deputy executive. But she has no influence on the decisions of the church.

I did not like Juliette when I first met her. She was aggressive and seemed to be at loggerheads with many of her colleagues. Employed as a senior development officer, Juliette's tasks were to assist the church in identifying and implementing development-related projects. Despite her initial coldness toward me, I got interested in this woman because of her peculiar job in the field of church development. Such jobs are rarely given to women. What was special about her? So I persuaded Juliette to let me accompany her on her field trip.

As we got to the garage, I expected to find a driver. But Juliette checked the large range-rover for all the things necessary for a long trip. Finally, she made sure that her emergency light had batteries, and then asked me to hop in the passenger seat next to her. Off we roared, onto the rough country roads with ditches and holes. The toughness of the roads and how Juliette handled them made me realize that she was a no-nonsense woman.

As we drove, we talked. I soon came to realize that Juliette's unpleasantness was a defense mechanism. A university graduate in agricultural science, Juliette has all the qualifications the church needed for her job. But many people objected to giving her the job because she was a woman. She had found that unfair and fought for it. After getting the job, the church wanted to divide Juliette's responsibilities into sections, and Juliette objected. Thus, Juliette is using all her energy to show that she is able to do the job. She has made tremendous progress. But the church sees her "fighting spirit" as indicative of a "lesser" woman. Therefore people try to find fault with what she does. When she got the job, the rules said that the development officer would have a car and a driver. It was not long before some members of the church started criticizing Juliette, thinking that she could be having affairs with the driver during the long trips they made together. Therefore, Juliette has refused to have a driver, even though she really needs one.

As we reached our destination, I saw a different Juliette. The people liked her; she was kind to them. She listened to their needs and offered advice here and there. As Juliette worked with the people I saw the project develop. I saw her listen to the wise old men and women. She very diplomatically spoke with the government agricultural representatives. The next day as we left to return to the church headquarters, Juliette talked about nothing else but people's needs. She wanted to reach out and open the ways for the church to help.

A few months later, I received a letter from Juliette. The development board was critical of her working style. They said that she was paying too much attention to small projects and women's projects. They wanted big projects like institutions. Juliette was heartbroken. But she refused to give up. She is still trying. Will she change the church or will the church change her? How long will her energy last? How long will she take the criticism? As I write this chapter, Juliette has just refused to get married because it would hinder her professional involvement. But the church thinks she should get married. Single women are suspect in the church in Africa! I have sometimes wondered why many of Juliette's male colleagues find fault with her. Could it be because they think that their friendliness will be interpreted differently by Juliette or the public?

•

These stories of African women in the church speak louder than words. Recently I was caught walking in the rain. All I had to cover my head was a basket. I removed my notebook from the basket and tried to protect it from the falling rain by putting it inside my clothes. Then I put the basket on my head. At first I felt safe. I felt that I had covered myself. But soon the water started to filter through the basket. I not only got soaked, but the basket became heavy and unpleasant to carry. How very similar to the situation of women who gain power in many churches in Africa. They get positions, but soon those positions are disempowered or they are so heavily laden with cares that the wish to remain in positions of power diminishes. Even worse, women in positions of power often find that they do not make an impact on the church. Many women in power positions are now beginning to name their powerlessness.

This new awakening is the realization that presence does not mean participation. In the decade of the 1990s African churches may be forced to take account of their actions. African women will either speak out in protest or keep silent in protest. Either way, their cry is for the power to participate with dignity, the power to name themselves, the power to celebrate true partnership in society and in the ecclesia.

The Spider's Web
of Triple Oppression

Jean Sindab

S he was black, she was poor, she was uneducated, a victim of
the triple oppression of racism, sexism, and classism. To most it
would appear *she had no power at all*. Yet she used the power that she
had, the power to say no, when she refused to give up her seat to
a white man on a segregated bus in Montgomery, Alabama, U.S.A.
Her name was Rosa Parks, and she is the mother of the civil rights
movement, the woman whose *no* unleashed the historic movement
that resounded around the world. But, most importantly, her defiant
no unleashed the power within her, and within so many of the oppressed groups within the United States, to challenge successfully
the most powerful country in the world to end the system of racial
segregation.

For poor, racially oppressed women, Rosa Parks was a role model
who had much to teach about the close analogy between racism
and sexism. Despite her historic role she was soon relegated to the
sidelines of the movement she launched. While she succeeded in
challenging racism, she fell victim to sexism in the civil rights movement, which attempted to render her powerless. Nowhere are the
linkages between racism, sexism, and classism more clearly seen than
within the context of a discussion of *power*. In this chapter I would
like to address three basic issues:

- how racism, sexism, and classism are related to the exercise of power
  and domination

- why women are powerless

- how we empower women within their churches and society at large.

Racism, Sexism, Classism and the Exercise of Power

Being a victim of triple oppression can provide particular insights into power: its use, its misuse, and its role in perpetuating an oppressive system of domination and in maintaining racism, sexism, and classism. Power is the ability to have control over one's life and community, to have decisions implemented, to resist the domination and repression exercised by others, and to have choices and alternatives in life. But what does it mean not to have power? Those without power are dependent on those who have it; their lives are controlled, manipulated, and determined by those with power; their choices and alternatives are severely limited, if not completely eliminated, by lack of power. Being a victim of racism and sexism basically means having no power. Institutionalized racism and sexism ensure that social, political, and economic structures are controlled by the powerful to the detriment of those who do not hold power.

The minutes of the 1980 Central Committee of the World Council of Churches (WCC) spoke of the relationship between racism and sexism:

> It has become progressively more clear that women are victimized even more than men are, most notably under the system of migrant labor and apartheid. The links between racism, sexism, and the role of theology in perpetuating both, require more profound attention.[1]

The linking of oppressions in the exercise of power results in inequality and injustice. The participants of the Sixth Assembly of the WCC in Vancouver recognized this triple oppression, declaring that "racism, sexism, class domination, denial of people's rights, caste oppression are all woven together, like a spider's web."[2]

Women, as victims of racism, sexism, and classism, are in a unique position to illustrate the links between the three and expose the power relations that characterize them. It is this triple oppression that shapes the social, economic, and political features of women's existence. It also makes it necessary for women victims to establish a particular political space for themselves that recognizes their unique political situation. They have to wage a three-front struggle for their liberation along the lines of race, sex, and class. The victims of this triple oppression are undoubtedly the most oppressed among the oppressed. Let us now turn to an examination of the basis for this triple oppression.

Institutionalized Sexism

The term "institutionalized racism" is an integral part of the vocabulary used to discuss racial policies and their impact. The term means racial discrimination and prejudice combined with the power exercised not only by individuals but social, political, and economic institutions as well.

Institutionalized sexism operates in exactly the same way as institutionalized racism. It strips women of power, dignity, and freedom. However, the term "institutionalized sexism" is not widely applied to describe the oppression of women. Many will not recognize the institutionalization of sexist policies. Yet institutions such as the church have, over long periods, established, maintained, and implemented policies that are designed to limit the participation, opportunities, power, and functions of women. The refusal to recognize and deal with institutionalized sexism results in an inability to see that the injustices and oppression of sexism are as severe as those of racism.

A concrete example is the new constitution of Namibia, which makes it a criminal offense to practice racism but not sexism. Namibia's constitution, which is one of the most liberal in the world and contains inclusive language, e.g., "he and she," calls for affirmative action to redress past discrimination against women and makes discrimination against them unconstitutional. However, by refusing to make sexism a criminal offense it denies that racism and sexism are *equally* detrimental to human beings.

In another example, women and men within the church find it difficult to have sexism, like racism, treated as a violation of God's commandments. Allowing women's full and equal participation in the life of the church is *still* a matter of public debate within many denominations. Although the struggle against racism is still alive in the church, few would use Scripture *publicly* to defend racist practices, yet it is common for the Bible to be quoted to justify sexist practices and to legitimize the continuing exclusion of women from full participation and power-sharing in the church. At the World Convocation for Justice, Peace, and the Integrity of Creation, in Seoul, Korea, March 1990, it had previously been agreed that there would be three covenants in the final document. However, when a fourth one on racism was added, there was not one dissenting vote. If the women at the convocation had organized to introduce a covenant on sexism, it is doubtful that the same kind of support would have been forthcoming.

People with power view it as a "zero-sum game": if you have it, I don't have it. Consequently, the powerful do not even understand the concept of "shared" power. For them "shared" means lost. Even when it appears that power is being given or shared with women, institutionalized sexism ensures that other power mechanisms are erected to *replace* that which was lost and to *dilute* that which was given. While we find many more women today in high-level positions within the church, it must be remembered that there is a difference between "high-level" and "powerful" positions. Institutionalized sexism operates to limit women's power even in what would otherwise be powerful positions. There is a limit to the extent that women are given an opportunity to make decisions that affect the fundamental transformation of the institutionalized church into a truly liberating body. When posts previously occupied by men are filled by women, the power base of the position changes. First, in many cases the power of the post is shifted away or decreased. Second, people within the institution tend to attribute less power to an office when it is held by a woman. Third, women often remain dependent on a male hierarchical structure to retain and exercise the power of office.

Institutionalized sexism operates to ensure that sexist attitudes are perpetuated, not by individual action, but by attitudes that permeate the institution, affecting the ability of women to bring about structural and meaningful change that would empower women and help end injustice.

Invisibility of Women

An African-American theologian, Dr. Jacquelyn Grant, addresses the issues of power, participation, and the invisibility of women in black theology. In attempting to explain why there are so few black women theologians, she argues that their invisibility in society makes it very difficult for them to participate in structures that would provide them with opportunities for theological training. Participation, she says, is not limited by women's intellectual capacity but by the division of labor forced upon them. She argues that this has significance not only for the field of theology but throughout social roles and structures. In commenting on a division of labor that gives men opportunities for access to power but keeps women in the domestic sphere, she says:

This means that black males have gradually increased their power and participation in the male-dominated society while black females have continued to endure the stereotypes and oppressions of an earlier period.[3]

Women often identify this invisibility as a primary problem in society at large and most *particularly* in the churches. This invisibility of women is maintained by their "assigned" positions. Grant provides us with some helpful insights:

> It is often said that women are the "backbone" of the church. . . . What they really mean is that women are in the "background" and should be kept there. They are merely support workers. . . . In many churches, women are consistently given responsibilities in the kitchen, while men are elected or appointed to the important boards and leadership positions. While decisions and policies may be discussed in the kitchen, they are certainly not made there. . . . The conspiracy to keep women relegated to the background is also aided by the continuous psychological and political strategizing that keeps women from realizing their own potential power in the church. Not only are they rewarded for performance in "backbone" or supportive positions but they are penalized for trying to move from the backbone to the head position — the leadership of the church.[4]

Invisibility is also exacerbated because when the power structure begins to include blacks, its male bias focuses on black *men*, and when it includes women, its racial bias focuses on white women. Consequently, the few positions of power and opportunities for participation are often dominated by these two groups while racially oppressed women remain for the most part invisible and powerless.

Lack of Allies

Given a reality where "all the blacks are men and all the women are white," racially oppressed women are often in a situation where they struggle alone. They have, therefore, found it necessary to articulate their struggle separately in order to demand from their men that antisexism become an integral part of the antiracism struggle. They also need to insist to the women's movement that antiracism be an integral part of the struggle for women's liberation. At the same time these women have had to ensure that they are not alienated from either group and that their articulation of their separate struggle is not exploited by the white male power structure. This necessity imposes an additional burden on racially oppressed women as they struggle for liberation. These women have had to struggle to conscientize both racially oppressed men and white women rather than alienate them and lose them as allies in their struggle. A black South African woman put it most clearly in explaining the necessity for women to organize separately:

> Independent women's forums should not aim at excluding men from the fight for women's rights. We must not attack black men. We must attack the enemy and they are not the enemy. Their sexist attitudes and treatment of women are a product of social history.[5]

Yet women have often been disappointed to find that the liberation, power, and freedom that their communities struggle for are often not extended to the women. Nowhere is this clearer than in the separate churches organized by racially oppressed groups. Most of these churches or other institutions of the racially oppressed are established by men, as an alternative to the racism prevalent in white institutions. Yet within the context of these newly established institutions, they neglect to provide opportunities for women to participate and exclude them from positions of power. This is also true of women's organizations, where white women occupy most of the positions of power. What both groups must come to realize is that their struggles for equality and justice can be strengthened and fully achieved only if they include the struggles of women who suffer from triple oppression. In her article, Dr. Grant quotes a South African theologian who has explored this issue and clearly affirms that:

> Black theology, as it struggles to formulate a theology of liberation relevant to South Africa, cannot afford to perpetuate any form of domination, not even male domination. If its liberation is not human enough to include the liberation of women, it will not be liberation.[6]

Racially oppressed men who struggle against the evil and heresy of institutionalized racism must also reject the patriarchy that is an integral part of that system and forms part of its systematic pattern of domination. If white women reject sexism, then they must reject racism, for together they form the mechanism for maintaining the powerful patriarchal system.

Empowering Women

In the church the word "empowerment" has become as important as the word "solidarity." Its overuse tends to negate its importance and render it almost useless in dealing with the powerlessness of women. To deal with the concept of empowerment we must first gain a clear understanding of what power is and how it is utilized within the church and other institutions. The question can be posed: has the church really dealt with what is necessary to empower women? Does it have the political will to implement a true empowerment program?

The church can best demonstrate its solidarity with women by becoming a strong advocate of their empowerment. By issuing strong, unambivalent challenges to sexist attitudes and behavior, it can begin to challenge the structures of power within its own institutions and other institutions in a way that powerless women never can. Church leaders can, in fact, inspire and motivate women and begin the process of empowerment. No oppressed group has more latent power and energy than women. The question the churches must seriously address is how to unlock it. Women are told both implicitly and explicitly by their families, their communities, their societies, and their churches that they are powerless. It could be argued, however, that it is the latent power that women possess, which could fundamentally affect structures and institutions, that frightens those who currently hold power. Unfortunately, sexism, like racism, operates to convince women of their inferiority, their powerlessness, and their dependency upon those who dominate them. Women are beginning to challenge their oppression, however, in increasingly strong ways. That process will continue. When a woman is confronted with blatant racism, most often she will challenge it; when confronted with blatant sexism, however, the challenge and the response are not always as quick. Cultural and social barriers sometimes act as a break. In such instances women act to disempower themselves.

As we approach the twenty-first century women will need more courage to insist that institutional sexism within the church be recognized as the same kind of evil transgression of the Gospel of Jesus Christ as racism.

It is absolutely essential to define clearly where power is lodged in the church and make attempts to have women in those positions. Women must establish support networks to enable themselves to struggle against institutionalized sexism.

Women have many opportunities for meeting on their own. Such opportunities need to be used wisely. Less time should be spent on community-building activities such as singing and dancing, and more on strategizing to increase women's participation so they can gain power within the church to affect their lives. Every opportunity can be an occasion for empowerment. Women must fully recognize their power and use it. Women need to stop concentrating all efforts on empowering others and start empowering themselves. The church today is one of the strongest, most powerful, and richest institutions in the world because of the human, economic, and social resources of women who comprise the majority of its membership. Women could begin to use those resources for themselves and to pressure the institutional church to share participation and power with them.

Women do have a certain amount of power, and that needs to be recognized: their critical role as mothers and educators is a chance to inculcate new attitudes, values, and social perceptions in children. Women must examine carefully the attitudes they are passing on in that capacity to ensure the development of nonsexist, nonracist, nonclassist attitudes in generations to come. Women must debunk the myths that keep them from obtaining, maintaining, and using power such as the belief that power is a corrupting force. In researching this chapter, I was not able to discover much on the subject of women and power. If women are to attain power, they must start preparing their own analysis of it. This is important for devising strategies for achieving power.

This chapter has drawn heavily on Jacquelyn Grant's article, because it is one of the few sources that clearly address the issues of racism, sexism, and power. Therefore, it is fitting that she should have the last word:

> If the liberation of women is not proclaimed, the churches' proclamation cannot be about divine liberation. If the church does not share in the liberation struggle of Black women, its liberation struggle is not authentic. If women are oppressed, the church cannot possibly be "a visible manifestation that the gospel is reality" — for the gospel cannot be real in that context.[7]

Notes

1. WCC Central Committee Minutes 1980–83, 60, WCC.

2. *Gathered for Life*, ed. Michael Kinnamon (Geneva: WCC, 1983), 86.

3. Jacquelyn Grant, "Black Theology and the Black Woman," *Black Theology: A Documentary History, 1966–1979*, ed. Gayraud S. Wilmore and James H. Cone (Maryknoll, N.Y.: Orbis Books, 1979), 420.

4. Ibid., 423–24.

5. *Women of Africa Speak Out*, ed. M. Mizuno and Jeane Becher (Geneva: WCC, Sub-unit on Women, 1989), 40.

6. Grant, "Black Theology and the Black Woman," 430.

7. Ibid., 423.

The Feminist Challenge

Ranjini Rebera

A nna is the mother of five children. She and her family live in a slum on the outskirts of Buenos Aires in Argentina. It is like any other slum, whether in Calcutta, Colombo, or Manila. Anna attended the workshop I was conducting on the theme "Women and Power." While every other participant was able to make time to live in the college where the workshop was being conducted, Anna couldn't afford that luxury. She woke up every morning at 3:00 a.m., did her housework, cooked, cleaned, and sent the younger children off to school, and then she and her sixteen-year-old daughter would take a two-hour bus ride to be at the nine o'clock worship session. After the evening session they would take another two-hour ride back to their home in the slums. They did this for five days. I visited Anna's home and the women's collective she runs. Anna has a burning passion to empower the women in her neighborhood. These women meet daily in a dilapidated room to cook a mid-day meal for about fifty children. By pooling their resources they make sure that their children have one fairly wholesome meal a day. Anna and her collective have the motivation to make a better life for themselves. They know they have some skills. They know there is more to life than the daily grind into which they are bound. But Anna's eyes were sad and angry as she asked me: Why? Why can't we make a better life? Is it because we are women? Or is there some other reason?

My friend Mano was a gentle, loving, deeply spiritual woman. She and her husband, Bala, and their two sons, aged fifteen and seventeen, left Sri Lanka at the height of the ethnic violence. They went to Singapore on a three-year assignment. Mano shared with me her deep anxieties for her sons — her agony of wondering who would get them first, the army or the terrorist groups. Her three years in Singapore were an oasis of peace for her. At the end of this time Mano and Bala returned to Sri Lanka. The boys were sent to Madras in India for further study. Bala got a job as principal in a school in the hill country. Late one night last year, there was a knock on their door. Mano and Bala walked directly into a hail of bullets. Mano died on the spot. Bala died two hours later. When the news reached me, I found anger — no, rage — the strongest emotion in me. All my sadness and sorrow at losing our friends were subsumed in rage. Why? What had these gentle people done? Was it they? Or was it the system? Was there individual blame? Or collective blame?

The last story concerns Maria, a young single mother. She is also a theological student in her final year of study. In September of last year Maria was invited to preach in a church she had never been to before. While she was delivering the sermon, Maria noticed a young woman creep into the church. Her face was badly bruised, and she was cowering in fear. She slipped into a pew and sat quietly. A few minutes later Maria saw a man appear at the door. He looked around, saw the woman, and sat down at the end of another pew. The young woman was shaking in terror. Maria acted spontaneously. She stopped her sermon, came down from the pulpit, walked to the woman, and put her arms around her and held her till the shaking stopped. After the woman had calmed down, Maria went back to the pulpit and finished her sermon.

Two weeks later Maria got a letter from her bishop asking her to meet with a ministerial committee. Maria went, not knowing why they wanted to see her. When she got to the meeting, she realized that she had been summoned for questioning. Why, asked her bishop, did she leave the pulpit in the middle of the sermon? How dare she do something like that? The questions and the accusations were many. Maria looked at me and asked: "Is this the church God is calling me to serve? Is the system more important than the woman who was being violated?"

I had no answers to Anna's questions nor to Maria's. For Mano it is too late. But I find myself asking the question again: *Why* is there injustice? Is it because we are women? Is it because it is imposed on us by society, or by individuals? Is it the system we have established within which society operates? If so, is a just society possible ... or is it a myth? The institutional church uses the term "just society" quite often, and I wonder if it now is nothing more than a phrase that has become part of the rhetoric of the church, or is there a genuine desire on the part of the church to establish a just society?

Economic Powerlessness of Women

Perhaps re-examination of the issues that contribute to economic injustice in the lives of women is a good starting point in trying to answer some of these questions. A United Nations report states:

> Women constitute half the world's population, perform nearly two-thirds of its work hours, receive one-tenth of the world's income and own less than one-hundredth of the world's property.[1]

In other words women have no economic status. Women, especially those in the lower socioeconomic group, live out their lives as "nonpersons" within the economic structures men have created and women have accepted. The labor women provide and any skills they possess are ignored or downgraded, not because they are redundant, but because the present economic structure does not place a high monetary value on unskilled labor, and certainly no value at all on domestic labor. Women toil from dawn to dusk in the home, in the fields, in factories, in shops, and in all manner of home-based trades to add to the income of the family or as the sole earners of a family.

> Many women work at home for factories — plaiting leather straps for chappals [slippers], fitting hair-clips on to metal strips, detaching plastic buttons, making bead-chains. In many ways this is the most insidious form of exploitation.[2]

Yet their earning capacity does not count in the larger economic structure within which society operates.

In rural areas women make up more than half the agricultural labor force. With the migration of men into cities in search of higher paid jobs, rural women are being left behind to look after the family and to work on the land. In the case of landless women, whose husbands migrate to the city or the Middle East for employment, many of them are forced into other areas of work to supplement their income. Such women become easy prey for the sweat-shops. With little or no education to fall back on, these women form the endless rows of workers in garment, pharmaceutical, and electronic manufacturing. After the meagerly paid work is over, women return to their families to cook, clean, nurture, and care for those dependent on them. The double burden of earning, or supplementing, the daily wage and bearing and rearing children is a never-ceasing occupation. Yet such women do not have any economic status. Work in the home is a "woman's job" for which there can be no pay. It is the role of a woman. How can such work be paid for? But work outside the home, even though it merits equal pay to a man's work, is classified as incidental, because it's something a woman does before she comes back home to her real job — domestic work. The economic system of the world would not be able to survive if domestic work done by women in their own homes became economically viable and a wage was attached to it. There are no trade union movements to assist women in these struggles. In fact, women have little representation in the decision-making processes of trade unions because most women cannot afford the time to attend union meetings after a day's work. I have yet to hear of large numbers of men unable to participate in trade union activities due to housework or the needs of the children.

Women in the middle-income group are in a different category. They have access through education and training to higher-paid jobs, or they have spouses who are able to earn a fairly decent wage, so they tend to see economic injustice in a different form. To some women, economic injustice manifests itself in the unequal wage system that exists in most countries. This is the system that accepts and often legislates a higher wage for a man, even though a woman may be trained and capable of doing the same work. The woman's skills may be equal or superior, but *because she is a woman* and for no other reason, she is relegated to a lower wage level. To other women, economic injustice manifests itself through the high cost of living that forces families to stretch the family budget to the maximum. When families can't make ends meet, women are forced to enter the workplace. Any education or skills such women possess can pave the way to a slightly higher wage, but never to the wage to which they are entitled. Once again the economic system slots women into a different category, purely on the basis of gender. Like their rural sisters, more and more women in the middle-income group need to find avenues for supplementary incomes because of the high cost of living in all Third World countries. These women may not have to face the dehumanizing work of a sweatshop. They may find it easier to get work in a shop, a bank, an office, or in teaching or nursing. But they will face the same exhaustion and the same exploitation that women in the lower income groups face. The demands on them in the domestic sphere remain the same. The unequal wage system will pay them less than their male counterparts. They have no recourse to justice, because most trade unions in our countries do not see women's jobs as important.

In times of crisis women's unpaid labor in the home takes on additional importance. As the traditional guarantors of family survival women are usually most burdened with the task of making ends meet in the fact of shrinking family incomes and drastic price hikes.[3]

But how do these global phenomena affect women such as Anna and the millions of other women in our part of the world? A woman from the Federation of Shantytown Wives in Bolivia comments:

> We housewives are always asking ourselves, what did we do that we have to pay this foreign debt? We've never eaten or dressed well, we do not have nice homes or medical care. We haven't benefited. Why are we the ones who have to pay? It doesn't seem right that hungry people should have to pay in order to keep the bank's profits up.[4]

Yes, it is women who face the most horrendous effects of the debt crisis. With governments needing more and more finances to service their debts, productivity has to increase. Women work longer hours to generate more income. It does not mean that they will benefit from this extra production work. It means that their labor is exploited to pay off the debt they neither benefited from nor incurred. With the mushrooming of factories for increasing productivity, women have emerged as a cheap, dispensable labor force. The exploitation they face is not only unjust, but is often inhuman.

From Bangladesh comes the story of a woman working in a garment factory. While ironing, a broken needle pierced her eye. For five hours the woman suffered with no treatment; the management would not release another worker to take her to the hospital because they would lose the work of two people during these hours. As a result of the accident, she had to wear glasses. The management then refused to take her back on the grounds that she now had to wear glasses. She needed her job. She gave up wearing her glasses. Today she is gradually growing blind.[5] There are thousands of women who could relate similar stories. These women have no options left. The burden of the double day, with longer working hours and less time for the demands of the home, form the reality within which they live. At the end of each long working day, women have to spend more hours in their search for food, for water, for fuel. The longer working day causes other changes in the lives of women:

- Cooking practices change. Quick, easy-to-prepare meals, usually of poor nutritional value, are produced once a day in bulk.

- Intra-family distribution of food is affected. Women have no time to supervise the distribution of food.

- Housecleaning, essential in overcrowded and unsanitary conditions tends to decline.

- Fuel and water collection is constrained by time.

- Care of children is relegated (even more) to other siblings and grandparents.[6]

Medical and educational fields are often the first to face the impact of budgetary controls. Countries in financial crisis do not hesitate to cut back on education, health care, and social services. In all these areas it is women who are the victims. The number of schools is reduced and the few schools maintained have to serve the needs of a larger number of children. Male children get preference over female children when school fees increase. With the decreasing availability of health and medical facilities, women and children become the first victims of these cuts. The rise in infant mortality in Third World countries in recent years bears testimony to the decreasing availability of these basic needs of women and children.

Children too pay the price for the debt crisis. UNICEF records that there are over nine million abandoned children in Brazil alone. These are not rebellious children who have run away from home. These are mainly children abandoned by a society that can no longer support them. To survive, the majority of these children learn the quickest trade that will bring them money: prostitution. Child prostitution is a serious problem in Brazil, in the Philippines, in Sri Lanka, in Australia, and in any country that is facing homelessness among its children and young people.

The impact of the debt crisis does not confine itself to the economic life of the countries of the South. It spills over into the life of all countries. It thrives on consumerism by creating markets to provide profit for those in control. It encourages corruption by welcoming into the coffers of international banks money that is siphoned off by corrupt officials in Third World countries and sent back to countries from which this money originated. It reinforces patriarchy by permitting the men who control the economic system to exploit and manipulate people, especially women, so that they can remain in power.

Patriarchy

It is easy to see the human face of patriarchy in oppression and the exploitation that women are subjected to in the economic areas of life. But when it comes to social issues, patriarchy can take many guises. From the rejection of the female fetus even before the baby is born to the giving in marriage, to the gender-specific role in a home, women know and experience the reality of patriarchy.

In Asian society there is still a myth that women are treated as goddesses and that motherhood is sacred. It is an image that should bring dignity and freedom to women. But the reality is the very opposite. If women are being treated like goddesses, how is it that our countries need to legislate to protect the rights of women? Why is it that despite such legislation, women have little or no property rights and women have little or no economic status in our countries? If motherhood is sacred, why are mothers treated with scorn and oppressed? Laws granting maternity leave in most countries do not state that this benefit is only for married mothers. But the practice discriminates between the wed and the unwed. Motherhood seems sacred only in the context of marriage, in other words, the protection of a man is required to sanctify the reproductive ability of women! Furthermore, the reproductive functions of women are still considered unclean. They serve one purpose alone: to give birth, preferably to a male child.

A society that, despite legislation, operates on the basis of patriarchy cannot be called a just society. Power resides with the powerful, and patriarchy is powerful. All the legislation in the statute books will not eradicate the control of patriarchy until women become aware not only of their rights, but also of the images and symbols they have inherited from childhood. Embedded in these images are the controls of patriarchy. "Girls are weak. Boys are strong." "Girls are silly. Boys are sensible."[7] And so it goes on. Interestingly, just as consumerism is targeted at women and is perpetuated mainly by women, so is patriarchy. We teach our children in the home, in our schools, through community activities, that male is superior, that male is right. Often we do this unconsciously because we have internalized these images from our childhood. Once these images are embedded in both women and men, it is inevitable that society reflects the same norms and principles. A grown woman believes she is weak and silly. A grown man believes he is strong and sensible.

A woman's low image of herself then becomes the source through which society exploits its women. Whether it be through economic exploitation or through social exploitation, the low image that most women have of themselves is crucial to the kind of acceptance women tolerate when social oppression takes place. Violence against women is a good example. With the rising level of consciousness created by women's groups, violence against women, especially physical violence, has come into the open. A start has been made. Rape is not talked of in the same hushed tones as in years past. But it is interesting that most laws governing rape still favor men rather than the victim, who is a woman. As Padmini Swaminathan writes, "Rape, not kidnapping and seduction, have been made offenses not to protect the person of the woman, but to protect the rights of a man against violation of another."[8]

This kind of violence, evident in countries such as Sri Lanka, gains its satisfaction through the raping and killing of women and children. Domestic violence in the form of dowry deaths and bride burning are other expressions of this form of violence. Dignity and the right to sovereignty do not seem to be valid for women. So gentle, caring women, like my friend Mano, become victims of violent societies that have grown to accept violence as the norm. Physical, economic, and psychological violence continues to form the fabric of our society. At a series of forums on "Violence and the Community" held in Canberra, Australia, an Asian woman talked of the pain of academic violence. She described the pain that women suffered in the name of academic advancement. Husbands pursue academic goals and academic advancement at the cost of family life and sometimes at the cost of a wife's career. Another form of this violence against women is evident in the fast-growing trade of prostitution.

Most societies still consider sexuality and women as synonymous. Sexuality is still linked to temptation and sin. Female sexuality has always been the property of men. A woman has no right to enjoy her sexuality; it is something she offers to the man. With this kind of imagery embedded in our psyche, it is not difficult to see how and why women become easy victims of prostitution. It is often the only way in which they can earn a living. When society closes the door to economic survival in the workforce, then a woman's body and her sexuality become the only tools of trade left. Today these realities are learned at increasingly younger ages. Young children, male and female, are encouraged to prostitute themselves in countries such as the Philippines, Sri Lanka, and Indonesia. In Thailand, prostitution is the second highest income earner of the country, next to the export of rice. Yet the woman who plies this trade is exploited at every step. Not only does she expose herself to venereal diseases, unwanted pregnancies, and illegal abortions, but today she runs the very real risk of contracting AIDS. Financially, too, she is exploited. The money she earns is seldom hers. What she gets is what's left over after her earnings have been divided among the night club owner, the tour operator, the local guide, and any others involved in bringing her business. The money she then earns could well be sent to the family she has left behind or to meet medical bills or to educate siblings. The majority of women who become prostitutes do so, not because they enjoy this kind of lifestyle (which is what most middle-class people like to believe), but because they have no other option for survival.

The hope for giving necessary protection to women who are forced into prostitution becomes slimmer as Third World governments look to tourism as the quickest way to earn much-needed foreign exchange. Prostitution is one of the "baits" on the hook that draws the tourists into a country to spend their dollars. The assumption is that tourists will empty their purses in our countries. The reality is that tourism benefits the tourist's country of origin as much as, if not more than, the country being visited. How does this happen? Take Thailand and the German tours that were prolific at one time. Most Germans would buy their tickets in Germany and travel on a German airline. Once in Bangkok, most of them would live in the larger hotels. These hotels would be furnished with imported furnishings so that the tourists' standards for comfort would be met. So companies in Japan and Taiwan benefit through the trade. Finally, the amount spent by the tourists in Thailand is rarely as much as the government would like us to believe. Therefore, neither social nor economic benefits result from prostitution or tourism. The stark reality is that social injustice and economic injustice seem to form the cornerstones of our society. The position of women in society is a sad indictment of our social systems. The old saying is proved true again: You can judge the degree of civilization by the social and political position of the women in that country.

The question then is, how does one build a just society, in which women share in the use and distribution of power? Do the Christian community and the institutional church have a role to play in building a just society? My young friend, Maria, standing before a group of male church leaders and being condemned for going to the aid of a victim of violence, doesn't see any hope for the institutional church and its role in building a just society. Women being called by God to serve as ministers of the Word and being denied that right in some churches, purely on the grounds of gender, do not see a role for the institutional church in building a just society. The institutional church, which seems to spend so much time and money in acquiring property, constructing concrete cathedrals, and conducting litigation, will not have the vision or the credibility to help construct a just society. Any institution that accepts patriarchy as its model and patriarchal images as its symbols and its vision will have little credibility in the process of building a just and equal society.

Hidden Power

To me the greatest hope for women lies in rebuilding and restructuring society through collective actions by women themselves. I believe that women can, and will, change society. That is not rhetoric. It is the reality and it is also the most logical direction for society to turn. This is beginning to happen. Let me share another story with you:

> Pavement dwellers always live in uncertainty and fear. A group of pavement dwellers in Bombay, India, heard of the forcible eviction of people to a site nearly 40 kilometers away. As they worried over their own fate, the women began to work out a strategy. With no education and certainly no literacy, these women began to develop a simple method for searching alternatives for living. They began to visit and check out possible locations into which they could move. They could not read maps, but they used symbols and signs to locate positions and sites. They finally worked out how much land they would need and began negotiations with local government authorities. The process still continues. But by being involved, by taking their own initiatives, by making decisions, these women have begun developing dignity and confidence. Above all, they have begun to see and experience the strength in collective action.[9]

By pooling their limited resources, Anna and her collective of women in the slums of Buenos Aires are making their resources go a long way as well as experiencing the strength of collective action.

Collective action is powerful and can change structures. Collectivity is not a new concept. It is evident in all societies throughout history. Collective action is the basis of the success of movements that have changed the course of history. Women in the lower socioeconomic groups are realizing the impact of collective action through self-help groups and cooperatives that are growing in number in Third World countries. Since women are still nonpersons in most economic systems and women's work outside the home is seen as secondary to their role as mothers and caregivers, the formation of collectives and self-help cooperatives empowers women gradually to rethink their own acceptance of roles. This awareness gives women the strength and the vision needed to challenge the structures that keep them imprisoned.

Collectivity has other offshoots. It strengthens the voice of women. A woman alone needs tremendous courage and resources to change her situation. Women together can articulate their needs more forcefully and more clearly. Satyarani, the mother of a victim of a dowry death in India, enlisted the help of a women's collective to fight for justice when the offender got off without punishment. When asked why she didn't organize a demonstration soon after her daughter's death, she said:

> I didn't know about these demonstrations. Otherwise I would never have let the hundreds of women of my community who came to mourn the death of my daughter sit around crying with me. We would have gone together and demonstrated outside their house, put pressure on the neighborhood to socially ostracize the family and got justice for ourselves.[10]

Satyarani is a leading organizer of antidowry demonstrations today, a woman who discovered the strength of collective articulation and collective action.

Collective action is often easy to accept within a situation such as economic or social oppression, especially in the lower socioeconomic level of society. It is harder for women who belong to the middle-income level. They have to contend with status, with custom, and with culture much more than women living in low-income communities. Most of them have been molded to believe that collective action is Marxist or feminist or even "unwomanly." I do accept that it is difficult for some women to take part in demonstrations and to align themselves with groups that lobby for social and economic reform. But this is not the only way to bring about a just society.

Women in the middle socioeconomic group are beginning to realize the need for being informed. They are beginning to learn that economics and legal issues are not for economists and lawmakers alone. They are beginning to realize that they need to know about the debt crisis, which is creating an economic structure that is exploiting them as well as those in the sweatshops and those exploited by social evils such as prostitution. Women are beginning to realize that they can analyze the teachings of patriarchal religions that would keep them under bondage. Women, more and more, are becoming aware of their own right to think for themselves and to make choices for themselves. Women are beginning to realize that being

vocal is not only demonstrating in street marches, but it is also taking a stand for themselves in the home, in the community, in the
work place, and in religious institutions.

Collective action empowers the individual as well as the total
group. It is a concept that is easy for women to grasp because we
have a natural ability to gravitate toward each other. We find it easy
to communicate with each other, to be open with each other. This
is an excellent foundation on which to build women's collectives
and women's networks.

Collective action is not only the prerogative of society outside the
church. It is so within the church as well. Unfortunately, until recent
years it has been hidden within layers of patriarchy. But it is there,
and women theologians and biblical scholars are beginning to recognize and articulate it. The Gospel stories record images of a strong
collective of women. The phrase "a group of women" appears many
times in the Jesus narratives. The strongest evidence of this group
was at the foot of the cross. The women stood in solidarity with each
other in a situation that must have been frightening and bewildering
to them. Their collective support empowered them to keep going
when there seemed to be no hope. Later, when the disciples refused
to believe Mary's report of her encounter with the risen Christ, a
group of women went back to the empty tomb. Women believing
in women. The growth of the women-church movement is the con-
tinuation of collective action within the church. Rosemary Radford
Ruether writes: "For the first time the vision of the church as an
exodus community from patriarchy is being developed by feminist
Christians."[11]

Reconstruction — The Challenge to Women

Economic and social systems built on patriarchal images and in patriarchal molds are destroying this planet. The global economic and
environmental crises affect the lives of all of us. It affects the lives of
the children who will inherit the world we hold in trust for them. We
have a responsibility to them, and we have a responsibility to each
other. That is what collectivity is about. Our lives and our actions
are interlinked, and unless each of us is committed to building a just
society, the process will be longer and more painful for all of us.

It is not my intention to polarize the sexes, to create an all female community and ideology. But I do believe that the strength of
women to change and create a just society lies in our ability to recognize our own gifts and strengths. Once we take that step, then we

need to support each other as we struggle to change the economic and social structures that hold both women and men in bondage.

Perhaps that is my answer to the questions raised by Anna and to Maria and to women like Mano, who continue to live in violent societies: that we keep alive the vision for realizing the wholeness. Perhaps this sounds like rhetoric. Phrases such as "changing society," "building a sustainable society," "building a just society" form a part of the language of today. Sometimes they do become rhetoric. But to me the most challenging feature of being a woman in today's world is that for the first time women are able to change the rhetoric to reality.

About five years ago, two young Indian men strayed into a rural women's workshop I was conducting. It happened through a process of miscommunication. With the permission of the group, however, the two men stayed for the five-day workshop. Just before the workshop concluded, one of them said (as earnestly and as fervently as only a young university graduate can), "Madam, socialism has failed India. Communism has failed India. I believe the answer for India is feminism." I replied, "Bless you, my son! Go, spread the message!"

The feminist reconstruction of our society is to me the strongest hope for our planet. The patriarchal model has failed. Matriarchy is not the answer either. But I believe that feminism can and must be taken seriously if a just society is to be built. If feminism becomes another ideology, it will fail as well. However, if feminism can continue to challenge patriarchal structures and provide alternatives at the same time, if feminism can lead to an honest analysis of patriarchy and an honest analysis of women's role in perpetuating it, if feminism can continue to help women develop new perspectives, not just about women and women's issues, but about any issues that concern human living, then feminism will never become another ideology or another "ism."[12]

Feminism has the potential and the power to reconstruct our society. By beginning with women's experiences and women's stories, by affirming the nurturing, the caring, the healing, and the dreaming that women bring to society, feminism challenges the structures that keep us imprisoned. It also challenges the acceptance of patriarchy as the norm for humankind. This is the vision and the challenge to which we, as women, are called today.

Notes

1. In Hannelore Schroder, "The Economic Impoverishment of Mothers Is the Enrichment of Fathers," *Women, Work and Poverty*, Concilium, ed. Elisabeth Schüssler Fiorenza and Anne Carr (Edinburgh: T. & T. Clark, 1987).

2. Rohini Banaji, "Organising Women at Work," *ISIS, Women's Journal*, no. 4 (September 1985), produced with the Committee of Asian Women.

3. Lynn Jones, "The Impact of the Debt Crisis on Women," *Resource Material on Debt* (Geneva: World Council of Churches Committee on the Churches' Participation in Development, 1988).

4. "Capital Flight: The Rich People Profit, the Poor People Pay," *WILPF* 53, no. 4 (December 1988).

5. Fazila Banu Lily, "Garment Industry and Its Workers in Bangladesh," *ISIS, Women's Journal*, no. 4 (September 1985), produced with the Committee for Asian Women.

6. Susan George, "The People and the Planet," *A Fate Worse Than Debt* (New York: Penguin Books, 1988).

7. Ranjini Rebera, *A Search for Symbols: An Asian Experiment* (Hong Kong: Christian Conference of Asia, Women's Concerns, 1990).

8. Padmini Swaminathan, "Legislation for the Improvement of the Socio-Economic Conditions of Women: The Indian Case," *Women in Development in South Asia*, ed. V. Kanesalingam (Delhi: MacMillan India, 1989).

9. Troth Wells and Foo Gaik Sim, eds., "Building Their Future," *Till They Have Faces: Women as Consumers* (Rome: ISIS International, 1987), reprinted from: *Lokayam Bulletin* 5, no. 5 (1986).

10. Miranda Davis, "Women, Politics and Organisation," *Third World, Second Sex* (London: Zed Press, 1983).

11. Rosemary Radford Ruether, "Redemptive Community," in *Womanguides* (Boston: Beacon Press, 1985).

12. Elizabeth Gross, "What Is Feminist Theory?" *Feminist Challenges: Social and Political Theory*, ed. Carole Pateman and Elizabeth Gross (Allen & Unwin Australia).

Scripture Can Empower Women

Open Our Eyes

Raquel Rodríguez

I t is not only good but also "right and proper" for Christians to seek strength, power, and understanding in the biblical message, to look to it for the enlightenment that helps us to "open our eyes" and truly enables us to open ourselves to understand and, with one another, to reflect on the task that has been entrusted to us.

Our problem, as women, basically is not that of total blindness in regard to the situation that confronts us on all sides. None of us, or perhaps it would be better to say very, very few of us, suffer from that malady. Our problem is like that of the Samaritan women (John 4:1–29, 39). Like her we have not opened our eyes *enough*. We see only part of what is in front of us, what is most obvious, most tangible, that affects us most directly. We have to open our eyes, or help each other to open our eyes, to a deeper reality, to see what lies beyond what we can see with the naked eye. Opening our eyes in this way allows us to be agents of change, transforming our reality, in the same way as the woman in the passage was able to transform her reality.

Let us approach this passage to discover the sources of light it can provide for the task of opening our eyes.

Jesus and the Samaritan Woman

First, we encounter two characters in the story.

According to the Gospel account, Jesus is on his way to Galilee and has to pass through the region of Samaria. He comes upon a well, a source of spring water, which tradition says is the well of Jacob. Jesus is tired and sits down by the well to wait for his disciples, who have gone in search of food. There he meets a woman who has come to draw water, and their dialogue begins.

Up to this point the passage does not seem strange or shocking when read in the context of our reality today. However, in its historical context, in the social and religious context of that time, it is practically a scandal. We are called to open our eyes to an underlying reality different from our own.

Let us examine those elements that convert this simple encounter into something scandalous.

Jesus is a Jewish man. She is a Samaritan woman. These two peoples, who had the same origin, were in conflict. The Jews considered themselves superior to the Samaritans because the latter group had fallen into the hands of the Assyrians. The Samaritans despised the Jews because they had destroyed their most important temple in the city of Gazirin (128 B.C.E.). Of course, the two peoples had not been worshipping Yahweh in the same temple. Each group had its own sacred mountain. Yet they shared a common origin: the patriarchs, Moses, and the Law. Also, both were awaiting the Messiah who had been promised to them. The prophet par excellence of the Samaritans was Hosea, who portrayed the problem of religious syncretism using the image of the prostitute wife.

Besides the ethno-religious problem, we are confronted by an act that was seen as scandalous in that society: a man speaking to a woman in public, a woman who, as we learn later in the text, doesn't have the best reputation in her community.

Opening Our Eyes to Jesus' Message

What reality does Jesus want to open our eyes to with this act that was so scandalous in the context of that time? I believe that he wants to open our eyes to the message of inclusiveness. None of us would want to believe that we have exclusive rights to the message of the life of the Reign of God. In so doing we would exclude those who we think should not be allowed to hear that message. The message of life of God's Reign is universal in the fullest sense of the word. We have not been called to predetermine to whom the message ought to be directed. Ethnic, ethical, sexual, or any other characteristics are not what God takes into account when pouring out God's love and grace on us.

This passage and others like it open our eyes to the reality that social, ethnic, religious, ethical, and sexist prejudices cannot be allowed to keep us from announcing the message of life, which has also been announced to us as women and which social constraints have tried to diminish or take away from us altogether.

To open our eyes to this Gospel reality, Jesus breaks through the traditional social barriers. He embodies the human condition in his state of dependency, in his desire to satisfy a basic human need: thirst. That he possessed two attributes that in that context would make him superior (being a man and a Jew encountering a woman and a Samaritan) does not take away from the fact that his thirst was a quality common to every human being. To be in this situation of lacking something so vital shows that we are all, as human beings, equal before God. Putting himself in a dependent position vis-à-vis the Samaritan woman, who could help him to quench his thirst, is a concrete expression of the breaking of barriers imposed by society.

The passage continues, recounting the dialogue between this woman and Jesus. He asks her for water. She is amazed that a man and a Jew is asking her for water. From there a dialogue ensues in which it would seem that each one of them is talking about something different.

Perhaps we would be able to understand this dialogue better if we were to open our eyes to what this well, and water itself, meant for both Jews and Samaritans.

Water, as we all know, is indispensable for life. We can survive without eating for long periods, but without water we wouldn't be able to survive much more than three days. In desert areas, sources of water are not abundant. Each spring or well is of great importance to the people who depend on it. Water is synonymous with life.

But, in addition, this particular well has a religious and historical connotation. It is the well of Jacob, the patriarch of both peoples. It represents a common historical tradition and a link with the God of life who protected them and brought them to the promised land. The well represents life in many different dimensions.

The Samaritan woman talks about the life that this well and its water represent for her and her people. In a way she mocks Jesus when he says that now, after having asked her for water, he is offering her water although he has no container with which to draw it from the well. In contrast with the woman, Jesus is speaking of a new dimension of life, also symbolized by the water. She has her eyes opened to life according to her tradition, her faith, and her history. Jesus invites her to open her eyes to another reality of life.

Jesus wants the woman to open her eyes to a possibility that until now neither her tradition, her society, nor her religion — all symbolized in the water in the well of Jacob — has given her. He uses the concept of water with all that it represents for the woman.

The woman is not blind; she can see and talk about the water. But she cannot see beyond the water that is right in front of her, the water that quenches physical thirst. She still has not opened her eyes to all the conditioning that this well, with its historical background of social and religious traditions, signifies for her.

Nevertheless, as soon as the woman opens her eyes to Jesus' announcement of a new possibility for a life that would allow her to realize herself as a human being, she is ready to leave behind all that would tie her to a life of death. Here is a real and lasting new way, no longer that of a life not fully realized. This is why she asks where she must go to obtain this "water." In so doing, she leaves behind and breaks with the well of Jacob and all the conditioning given by her tradition.

The passage also opens our eyes to see that if we want to pass from a life conditioned and devalued by historical events on to a life fully realized, this cannot happen in a vacuum. Taking such a step implies a break with the past that first has to be mediated by our recognition of the concrete reality that must be faced before we can make that break. Opening our eyes to the reality, recognizing it, gives us the power to take that step. For this reason the dialogue between Jesus and the Samaritan woman changes abruptly, and we might ask why Jesus involved himself in this woman's private life at that precise moment.

Exegetes have made exhaustive studies of this passage. It seems to me that we can understand this part of the dialogue better if we understand that, as a result of the Syrian occupation, Samaritans worshipped five different gods, one of whom was Yahweh. This woman's five husbands (and the implication that the man she is with now is not really her husband) could symbolize the situation of religious syncretism that existed. Jesus wants to open the woman's eyes to the reality that, in the same way that she comes to the well to satisfy her thirst, her list of "husbands" symbolizes her search for a way to satisfy her desire for a full life. But none of the husbands has been able to accomplish this. It is this concrete reality with which she must break. It is not enough to say that she would no longer go to the well. She must also break with all that the well represents.

Opening Our Eyes to the True God in Love and Service

Immediately, the dialogue between Jesus and the Samaritan woman takes another turn. When Jesus speaks to her about her past life, without her having mentioned it, she recognizes him as a prophet: one she cannot accept because he is Jewish. Although until this point she has been opening her eyes to the deeper realities, here the conditioning of her historical and religious traditions returns to cloud her vision. She returns to her concept of the relationship between herself and God as an act of religious ritual. She has not really understood the image that is evoked by the "spring of life-giving water."

Jesus wants her to open her eyes to her need to break with her conception of encountering God as well. He opens her eyes to the reality that it is no longer ritual, but true worship that allows one to encounter the true God. He wants her to see that this comes out of a concrete relationship with others in love and service, because it is in that context that God can truly be found. That is what it is to worship in Spirit and in Truth, or as one modern version of the Bible says, to worship in an authentic way, in keeping with the Spirit of God. Love and service will come to be substituted for the old relationship with God, which was based on sacrifice, humiliation, and religious ritual. The relationship and the encounter with the God of life are to be found in this Spirit of life, in the struggle to achieve that life for ourselves and for others. Thus, the woman is being called to a life of full realization. To be able to participate in the new life she will have to break from the former relationship and begin a new relationship with God. That new relationship is to be seen in her announcing, and facilitating the new possibility of life for other people around her.

Even with all the clues that the Samaritan woman has been given by Jesus, she resists opening her eyes fully to the reality that is "right in front of her eyes." Perhaps the conditioning that she has experienced over so many years keeps her from opening her eyes completely to the reality that Jesus is "he who would come." But Jesus believes that now is the time to help her open her eyes completely. He gives her that last little push and reveals himself to her as the Messiah. He says, "I am he, I who am talking with you."

We could say from the way in which the dialogue has been going that it is quite likely that the woman had known for some while that she was speaking to the Messiah, but wanted to be on the safe side and preferred that he should say it first. She has just opened her eyes, but it's possible that she is afraid that because she is a woman, and a Samaritan, he will not confirm her great revelation. She still has not broken totally with the barriers of her tradition and her society.

Jesus, by revealing himself openly, allows her to break with these last barriers. As a result, she leaves her water jug cast aside to go and tell her people about the reality to which her eyes have been opened.

The water jug symbolizes her relationship to the well, and the well her relationship with her tradition. The woman has just broken away from all that to embrace the possibility of full life in the Reign of God announced to her by Jesus. That she communicates the message to her people by asking them "Could he be the Messiah?" doesn't mean that she still isn't sure of the truth. Rather she hopes each of them will take the opportunity to open his or her eyes to the revelation of the Messiah. She wants to help those women and men to have the same opportunity that she has had.

Our Relationship with the Samaritan Woman

Now, after discovering this message through which Jesus opens the Samaritan woman's eyes, you may be asking yourselves, "What does all this have to do with us?" A great deal, I believe.

We have been called to open our eyes to very concrete realities that are to be found all around us. For many of us this may be one of the first opportunities offered to us really to open our eyes.

Our cultures and our traditions have reduced our opportunity to live full lives as human beings. Our possibilities for living a full life have been limited by a patriarchal concept of society in which women are discriminated against because of their gender. We are women, therefore we are inferior. Church structures have not been exceptions in this discrimination.

But many of us come from countries where entire populations are also denied the possibility of living a full life. These are people overwhelmed by extreme poverty, incorrectly referred to as "on the road to development," because the process is not taking them forward but backward, and many of our people are in a worse situation now than they were twenty years ago.

Many of us also come from countries that are highly militarized, where the threat of death is constant and inescapable for each person who lives there. With death lying in wait, when we are looking down the barrel of a gun, how can we think that there could be a possibility of opening our eyes to an abundant life?

We all come from countries where, in one way or another, the problem of the external debt makes it difficult, and in some cases impossible, to think of possibilities for abundant life. Because this debt was created and promoted by the international economic system, there is no escape from its outcome.

In addition to this, we have all felt the effects of the degradation of our environment, which was created by God for the benefit of all humanity. We continue to feel the effects of this apparently limitless destruction, and those effects make us realize that the chances for a full life in a contaminated environment grow less every day.

All these situations mean that we live in societies in which violence is the most common way of relating to one another. Our societies are characterized by asymmetries: marked differences within the society on the basis of race, class, gender, or some other distinction. Violence is exerted against those persons who are part of the group considered inferior. Some of us come from the Third World and see how whole populations are discriminated against. We feel the violence inflicted in so many ways on all our people. But, as women, we recognize that those who are most under attack in this system are women and children. With so much violence in the world, and with new manifestations of violence occurring all the time, the possibilities for abundant life are very few, not to say almost nonexistent. Faced with these realities, we are called together to open our eyes.

Our responsibility is very great, because, since we have received the grace of the love of God, we are committed to being proclaimers of the message of the full life of God's Reign. Jesus Christ reveals to us the message of the full life as he did to the Samaritan woman. Ours is the responsibility to run as she ran, to proclaim the message, so that others may have the opportunity to quench their thirst for a life with real possibilities.

It is our responsibility to let all humanity know that this message of full life is universal and excludes no one because she or he is "different." It is a message that breaks through the barriers of asymmetry and announces the possibility of full life for each person, whether man or woman, old or young, black or white, native or non-native, able-bodied or disabled, rich or very poor, marginalized or socially acceptable. We do not hold the power to decide who has the right to live a full life and who only has the right to survive.

But it is very difficult to proclaim a message of abundant life when all around us the only thing being proclaimed is death. To be able to proclaim life we have to be able to know our concrete reality so that we can break with that reality and proclaim that we can now begin to drink the water that truly satisfies our thirst.

To break with that concrete reality is not easy. It is not enough to leave behind the water jug as the Samaritan woman did. It is not enough to say that we no longer accept poverty or the external debt or militarism or the destruction of the environment, nor to say that we want the violence against women and children to end, nor to say that discrimination against women must end. These by themselves would not put an end to the problems. It would be closing our eyes to reality.

Neither can we be content with the easy traditional responses: the poor are poor because they are lazy; women bring violence upon themselves by provoking men; corrupt governments steal the money that comes into poor countries and leave them in debt; the ecological situation can be solved by planting a tree. We need first to open our eyes to concrete situations, look for the root causes that have given rise to these situations of injustice and death, and then direct our energies to the search for solutions that may be able to turn these situations around.

If we do not complete this task, then the same thing that Jesus described to the Samaritan women will happen to us: we will have to keep returning to the well to satisfy our thirst, because easy answers or just wishing the problems didn't exist will not be sufficient to reverse the process of death.

We have acquired a responsibility because we have received the grace and love of God. Our responsibility is similar to that which the Samaritan woman acquired when her eyes were opened and the message of the full life of God's Reign was revealed to her. She ran to bring the message to her people.

It is time to begin the process of opening our eyes. It has been revealed to us that the way we can give thanks to God for such infinite grace is not by means of rituals, but by love, through serving others in concrete form. "The time is coming, in fact it is already here" when we are asked for proof of our gratitude to God. It is time to worship God "in an authentic way, in keeping with the Spirit of God." We can begin to do this by serving our sisters and brothers around the world, by opening our eyes to the situations that prevent the coming of the Reign of life, by denouncing those situations and by searching for concrete solutions that can help to overcome injustice and death.

It will be the responsibility of each of us to leave behind the water jug that ties us to whatever social, historical, or religious traditions keep us from being agents of transformation in our society. In encounters with the situations experienced by other women and other peoples and cultures, we will have a unique opportunity to open our eyes to the concrete reality of our universe and to search together for solutions to our problems.

This is the well of the encounter of the Samaritan woman with Jesus. Jesus Christ makes himself present here and calls us to open our eyes. We come with the water jug in our hands and all that it represents. In this encounter with Jesus Christ, it will be our responsibility to leave the water jug and go out to proclaim the new possibilities for life.

The Dance of Liberation

Violet Cucciniello Little

Some call the story in Luke 13:10–17 the story of the "bent-over woman":

> Now he was teaching in one of the synagogues on the Sabbath. And there was a woman who had had a spirit of infirmity for eighteen years; she was bent over and could not fully straighten herself. RSV

For eighteen years all she could see was dirt. There had been different kinds of dirt, it was true; but it was still dirt. Sometimes the dirt was dry and dusty, filling her lungs and making her choke. Sometimes the dirt was muddied and thick, coating the feet of all who passed her by. Sometimes the dirt smelled of human waste and animal waste, making it difficult not to vomit the small amount of bread she had managed to swallow. For eighteen years, all she could see was dirt; and with each day that passed, she could feel herself move closer to becoming part of the very dirt that had so covered her world.

Her body was twisted and bent; her eyes looked always into the dirt. But she remembered a time, so long ago now, of white desert flowers and skies bursting with the lights of the heavens. She remembered a time, so long ago now, of happiness in children's eyes, and babies sucking hungrily at their mother's breasts. She remembered a time, so long ago now, of love and possibilities, another's touch, and the warmth of human relationship. But that was a time so long ago now, and for eighteen years, all she could see was dirt.

> And when Jesus saw her, he called her and said to her, "Woman, you are free from your infirmity."

In silence she suffered for eighteen years feeling only shame in her affliction. Her twisted body could only be a curse from God, a judgment for some unknown wrong. No sound of complaint came from her lips; she filled her mouth with only the daily rhythm of her prayers. But hard as she tried, the woman could not control the ever-present ache in her heart. It happened on the Sabbath day, outside the synagogue where Jesus was teaching, that from the depths of an aching and a broken heart came the suffering cry of the beggar.

Standing Straight

That day was hot. The dust had already begun to fill her nostrils. Feet passed her by, as usual, kicking even more dirt in her tired and beaten face. Then, as if stopped by the cries of her broken heart, she saw the feet before her. The feet were strong and deeply tanned, calloused, having walked for many miles.

And then she heard a cry. Moving from a place so deep within his spirit he called her. The bent-over woman was free. She was made free by Jesus the teacher, Jesus the healer, Jesus the liberator:

> And he laid his hands upon her, and immediately she was made straight, and she praised God.

His hand touched her, and she was no longer alone. Drawn by the connecting touch of the Liberator, she was filled with a power that she had never known. The sound of the Liberator filled her ears. Slowly her eyes moved upward. She became tall; and arms once hanging only inches from the dirt began to reach high for the mysteries of the heavens. Not knowing what she would see once she left the familiar though suffocating way of the dirt, the woman trusted the Liberator and responded to his call. With body erect and arms moving to grasp all the wonders of creation, the woman began to praise her God.

> But the ruler of the synagogue, indignant because Jesus had healed on the Sabbath, said to the people. "There are six days on which work ought to be done; come on those days and be healed, and not on the Sabbath day."

But wait. There was yet another sound mixed in with the voice of the Liberator. It was the sound of one who had not seen the miracle. It was the sound of one who had not yet heard the voice of the Liberator. Could this be the sound of yet another whose world was lost in the dirt?

> Then the Lord answered him, "You hypocrites! Does not each of you on the Sabbath untie his ox or his ass from the manger, and lead it away to water it? And ought not this woman, a daughter of Abraham whom Satan bound for eighteen years, be loosed from this bond on the Sabbath day?"

The dance of the woman could be stopped by no one. And as she danced she heard the voice of the Liberator, clear and strong, challenging the leaders of the synagogue. "Daughter of Abraham" he called her. Daughter of Abraham. Suddenly the woman felt the joy of relationships she had once known. She felt the miracle of who she was in the ongoing story of God's saving history.

There was something else she learned from the Liberator. She learned her suffering was evil; it was Satan who bound her, but she was freed by the God who heard the cry of her aching heart. The God who called her to life was the God who suffered with her even when her eyes could see nothing but dirt.

> As he said this, all his adversaries were put to shame; and all the people rejoiced at all the glorious things that were done by him.

When Jesus the Liberator had said all there was to say, some left the temple, eyes moving toward the dirt. But the woman, made straight by the healing touch of Jesus and his proclamation of her freedom, touched those around her. And all began to join in the dance of praise, rejoicing together in the glorious things that Jesus had done.

The story of the woman bent over is a story of hope, challenge, and celebration for all who are part of the community of faith. Jesus, in the midst of teaching in one of the synagogues on the Sabbath, taught a powerful lesson through his interaction with the bent-over woman. Though we hear no words spoken by the woman, Jesus knows of her suffering and hears the cries that could only have come from her heart. He calls her and liberty is proclaimed. Then he touches her, and in so doing pulls her into a relationship with all humanity. No longer is she to be passed by on the roadside, face buried in a cloud of dirt. The woman has responded to the call of Jesus, risking the security of the world she has known and daring to face the challenges of the world around her. She responds to the call in faith and is empowered by the one who has called her. The joy she knows can only take shape in praise.

But the ruler of the synagogue did not see the miracle that had occurred before his eyes. Rather, he became so buried in the laws of the Sabbath that the time of rejoicing turned into a time of indignation. Jesus calls all who question his action "hypocrites." Priorities are set straight; care for one suffering human being takes precedence over care for other matters. Then Jesus calls the bent-over woman a "daughter of Abraham." She is not a child of Abraham nor is she a son of Abraham; the bent-over woman is a *daughter* of Abraham, recognized for who she is both as a woman and in relationship to those before her in the history of salvation. What is more, Jesus recognizes her suffering for the evil that it is; she is "bound" by Satan. The life of oppression is not the world as God intended it to be. The passage concludes with the adversaries of Jesus being shamed, while the others rejoice at the "glorious things that were done by him."

Healing for Today

In reflecting upon the situation of women in the church it is helpful to enter the world of the bent-over woman. Have women been so weighed down by their infirmities that they dare not see beyond the world of the dirt? Do women recognize sexism for the evil it is? Or have we women so internalized the misinformation of a sexist society that we either fear to cry out or do not hear the cries of other women? When women hear the call of God, do they respond? Or do they find comfort in the familiarity of their lives, even at the cost of pain and exclusion? What about the healing of Jesus? When women feel that touch, do they share it with others? There is a deep comfort in the assurance of a God who hears the cries of those who suffer. Those who know that God listens are called to respond to the voice of the Liberator in faith and thanksgiving.

The community of faith includes men. All are asked to enter the world of the bent-over woman. What is the response when a sister, once bent over, stands erect? Does the whole community rejoice? Or does it contribute to that which pushes her face in the dirt? Is the community of faith able to recognize the miracles and gifts that women bring to it? Does the community dare to share in the dance of celebration and praise, even at the risk of alienation and ridicule by others?

Like the woman bent over, women in the church cry both in agony and celebration.

Do church structures enable women in all cultures to stand with bodies untwisted, gifts waiting to be shared? Or are our church structures so lost in a world of legalism and control that they overlook those human beings who suffer exclusion and need?

The church's structures often do not allow women to make full use of their gifts and talents. Despite the biblical and theological realities of being claimed as God's own and saved by grace for Christ's sake, through faith, a broken and sinful humanity has continuously attempted to deny the identity given to women by God. Women have often experienced a sense of low self-esteem, allowing the false information put forth by a sexist society to become part of their own belief.

Women have lost trust in women. The effects of a patriarchal society have hurt women in many unknown ways. The challenge for women is to rejoice in their identity as daughters of God and members of the body of Christ. The challenge to women is to reach out to our sisters despite the misinformation each sister may have absorbed. The challenge to women is to meet our sisters wherever they are on their journeys and to walk with them in gentleness, mercy, and strength.

It is important for all to know that as part of the one body of Christ, we need one another. If one part of the body is sick, there can be no health. When women lose a sense of who they are within the communion, the message of the Gospel becomes distorted. It is God who empowers women to work toward justice, not any human being, not any human structure. But as women and men defined by the same living God, we must realize our connectedness in a way that truly manifests the revolutionary message of the Gospel.

God has promised to hear our cries: let's listen to each other's cries.

Missing Persons

Constance F. Parvey

In December 1981, I organized a conference for the World Council of Churches on the community of women and men in the church and the authority of Scripture. The meeting was held in Amsterdam, the Netherlands, and was attended by an international, ecumenical group of biblical scholars and students of the Bible, about forty in total. The issues we dealt with then have not disappeared, gone away, or been resolved. We are still struggling with the questions of justice for women in the Bible, the church, and the societies and cultures in which we live.

In 1981 these were the questions with which we struggled:

- Can the Bible, which has so many oppressive texts against women, be authoritative over women's lives?

- How can the few positive models of courageous women in the Bible compensate for the overall negative teachings, which portray women as being subordinate to men and the source of evil in the world?

- Would it be possible, or desirable, to create a new canon of the Bible that included only positive texts about women?

- Is there something like a "canon within the canon" of the Bible, i.e., positive teachings about women that could be the measuring rod by which all other biblical texts are measured and judged? For example, could this text become a measuring rod?

  > As many of you as were baptized into Christ have clothed yourselves with Christ. There is no longer Jew or Greek, there is no longer slave or free, there is no longer male and female; for all of you are one in Christ Jesus. (Gal. 3:27–28)

- Are women's experiences today so different from those of women 2000 to 3000 years ago (when the Scriptures were put into written form) that the Bible has little relevance for women's lives today?

- On the assumption that we, as women today, have achieved more equality than our biblical sisters, should we begin to read the Bible using our own contemporary experience? Perhaps we have something to give to the interpretation of Scripture, not only to receive from it.

- Is the Bible simply not relevant to women's lives today and to the new community of women and men emerging globally in our societies and in many of our churches?

The Captivity of the Bible to Patriarchal Structures and Mentalities

A patriarchal reading of the Bible has been a way that the Bible has been used against women by authorities in the church and society to justify certain views about women. The idea that women must be submissive to their husbands "to fulfill the law of Christ" has been used to justify violence against women's minds, bodies, and spirits. Even today in my own pastoral counselling with women and in shelters for battered women, women can be heard to say: "I had no choice. He is my husband; he has the right to beat me."

Many say that women should keep silent in the churches. This is because St. Paul seems to have written this at one moment to one church in response to a specific problem:

> Let a woman learn in silence with full submission. I permit no woman to teach or to have authority over a man; she is to keep silent. For Adam was formed first, then Eve. (1 Tim. 2:11–13)

This text has been used to exclude women from participating in the decision-making councils of the churches, and it has excluded women from theological education.

In 1955, I was one of the first women to enter the Harvard Divinity School. That is a little over thirty years ago, yet Harvard has already celebrated its 350th anniversary. This means in simple terms that for 320 years, women were not allowed to study theology there. For that matter, at that time in seminaries where women could study they were only allowed to study Christian education to teach children, not adults.

It is often said that women are not suited to the ordained ministry. Many churches do not ordain women. Even though some progress has been made, the argument about biological differences has not gone away. Roman Catholic and Orthodox women, among others, though they may now study theology, cannot be ordained because they are told by the hierarchy of the church that they do not bear the "image of Christ." These patriarchs interpret the image of Christ as exclusively male. They see this as the precedent for a male priestly tradition. Thus, the only way for women to be ordained is to have a sex change.

Women are seen to be responsible for original sin — they are the metaphor of evil. From the beginning chapters of the Bible to its end, women are the source of sin. In Genesis 2, it is Eve who is blamed for the fall of humanity and in Revelation 18, it is the whore of Babylon who must be overcome by the lamb of God. For example:

> Come out of her, my people,
> so that you do not take part in her sins,
> and so that you do not share her plagues;
> for her sins are heaped high as heaven,
> and God has remembered her iniquities.
> Render to her as she herself has rendered,
> and repay her double for her deeds;
> mix a double drought for her in the cup she mixed.
> As she glorified herself and lived luxuriously,
> so give her a like measure of torment and grief.
> (Rev. 18:4–7 NRSV)

These examples are some reminders of the injustices that have been, and still are being, perpetrated against women. Yet we live a paradox. Having rehearsed these themes familiar to us all, the paradox is that women are still here. Perhaps much of the reason for this is that women have over the centuries built "women church" in women's organizations in the churches. They have created for themselves survival structures and spaces within the patriarchy of the churches, and, because these have had a quality of invisibility, women have survived. Today, women make up almost 80 percent of the faithful Christians who attend worship regularly and who submit themselves regularly to these unjust readings of the Bible and to the consequent unjust preaching on its texts. This is no small injustice. It is a sin of the churches and of all those who have been complicit with it. But Christians know that they can confess their sins, be forgiven, and go on, and so they will.

The question for women of faith today is how can they be rooted in a biblical tradition that has done them such grave injustices and that has led many women to leave the church and fall away from the faith?

Women as the Remnant of the Remnant People

The Bible has been held captive to its cultures. The church too has been held captive to the patriarchal structures in its social setting. This is the sociology of our theology. Neither the multiple cultural contexts of the Bible nor the patriarchal structures of the churches are God-given. They are not designed by God. They are not part of the coming of God's Reign, of that which is and is yet to be. They are, rather, part of the man-made kingdoms of this world, of powers and principalities that rise and fall, come and go. The oral traditions of Scriptures were collected, recorded, saved, and interpreted by men living in male-dominated societies. From the very beginning of our biblical history in its written form, only remnants of women's lives and their experiences are recorded. The Bible is about a remnant people and women are a remnant within a remnant.

The good news is that women are present in the Bible from the beginning to the end. But the bad news is that they are mainly invisible. As women are so invisible, a great deal of time and effort has to be used to locate them as the remnant of the remnant. There is great joy discovering the strong women in the Bible and in finding texts that affirm women's equality in God and in Christ. But more than this needs to be done to make women more visible in the Bible. It is known that when the record was written, women were simply edited out of the script. That does not mean that God edited them out. No. It is those patriarchally shaped people with patriarchal mentalities, those who did not consider it important to include women, who rendered women invisible. The point, however, is not to blame anyone, but for women to own their invisibility and to reclaim themselves, their lost sisters, their lost traditions, and their lost stories of the women who birthed them into being over the centuries. The past is the past; what is important is the present and how it is used. It is known from numerous stories in the Bible, and in the life of Jesus that the Reign of God that Jesus ushered in, is always described as a quality of life where injustices are wiped away. In the Reign of God, all structures of domination are over-turned and all are invited to live a new equality of life with God and with one another. As the prophet Jeremiah said:

> But this is the covenant I will make with the house of Israel after those days, says the Lord: I will put my law within them, and I will write it on their hearts; and I will be their God, and they shall be my people. (Jer. 31:33)

In the Reign of God we are "heart people." What we experience of the Reign of God, when we experience it, are those qualities of the heart — compassion, justice, sharing, faith, hope, and love.

Recovering Women's Visibility in the Bible

How do women make themselves visible when long ago their traces and tracks were erased? Here are some clues. It is not easy, but it is not impossible. It takes some imagination and getting in touch with one's own experience.

- *Imagine that the text was written by a woman.*
  Put yourself in the center of the text as the writer. How would the most empowered part of a woman tell the story? Since the text was written from a male-centered perspective, it will have to be recreated as woman-centered. This does not mean changing the point of the text. What is added is another perspective, one that has been lost and must be recovered.

- *Remember that the text is written in telegraphic style.*
  Biblical texts are not normally long, drawn-out academic essays; they do not say everything. The writers tried to say what they thought was sufficient to get their point across. They edited. The text should not be changed, but enlarged, enhanced. The invisible woman actor is being added to the drama of the text.

- *Redeem the text for women.*
  Remember that every biblical text can be dangerous for women's minds, bodies, and spirits. The words and ideas used may make women feel insignificant and diminished.

- *Look for the women who might have been in the original oral story.*
  Use your sociological imagination, your everyday experience. Women have had similar roles across the centuries and across many cultures. Ask yourself, where are the mothers, the sisters, the mothers-in-law, the aunts, the wise women teachers, the healers, etc.

- *Imagine what the women might have said, might have done.*
  Look carefully at the concrete situation and imagine how a woman might have approached this problem, or this issue or situation.

- *Where are the women in this text today?*
  Ask, "Hello, are you there?" How does the present context of particular women enhance or inform the message of this text for the lives of women in different contexts?

- *Who is missing?*
  After you have found the women in this text, look for who is missing,

especially look for the poorest of the poor women, the most vulnerable women. How would they approach this text? What would be their contributions? What would be their fears and their hesitations, their expectations and their hopes? Every individual should then ask, "How do I see myself in them?"

- *Open your eyes.*
  How do you see the new community of women and men in this text?

Using these clues it is possible to explore a passage such as the prodigal son (Luke 15:11–32). This is a story with no women in the text; the characters are the father and two sons, the younger and the older brother.

The task is to discover the mother of the two sons. We cannot be sure that there were any sisters, but surely there was a mother. Where is she? Who is she? What part did she play in bringing up her children? Was she consulted in any of the events of the story? What might have been her counsel? What might have been her relationship to her two sons, or her husband? What could her name have been? How would you recognize or picture her in your own context?

The task is to make the women visible. It is part of redeeming time. Like the context in which this story is set, there is great joy in heaven when that which has been lost is found. The doing of justice in our community is a task of reclaiming women, time, history, continuity, and discontinuity with what has gone before, thus making the Bible relevant today — finding that which has been lost.

The Old, New Visions

Bärbel von Wartenberg-Potter

We long for a new vision in our desperate and difficult world. The worldwide community of faith needs a new vision. More than ever we live in a haze and the future looks dark. We hear the cry of the people everywhere, and every day one species of animal or plant life is extinguished from earth forever. What mother earth has brought forth is dying a slow, suffocating death. Clouds of nuclear annihilation are hovering over the world. Ghettos are filled with the agonies of the victims of racism, exploitation, and violence.

Yet at the same time, humanity has never had so many possibilities, so much power, so much money, so many goods, so much knowledge. Satellites are crossing the boundaries of our solar system. But the human heart has not grown in goodness, love, responsibility, and strength.

The cries of the people are louder now than ever before in history because the media portrays these contradictions for everyone. Sometimes even in beautiful colors. Who can absorb and comprehend the blood, despair, and brutality covering the earth and caused by human hands?

Where in the midst of all this is the sign of promise, the possibility for a new vision?

The Succession of Biblical Women

For a new vision we might have to go to old pathways and search for the witnesses of God's promise and hope in ages past. The new vision might indeed be an old vision. It might be given to a slave people in Pharaoh's Egypt and carried through by small and faulted people. Or it might be the vision made incarnate at Bethlehem and brought forth from the darkest hour of humanity, the hour of God's death at Golgotha and carried through to Easter morning in the garden.

Indeed, the new vision is the renewed old vision of a redeemed humanity, a redeemed world, bearing the "fruit of righteousness" in love and justice.

One of the great inspirations for women has been the song of Mary — the Magnificat. This is often reduced to pious devotion, but it must be recovered because it contains that old, new vision.

The Magnificat is to be found only in Luke's Gospel (Luke 1:26–38). Mary has not been prominent in Protestant theology. But we cannot neglect her any longer as we try to recover our biblical roots as women. We need to meet her as another Mary, not the Mary of Mariology, but as Mary of the Magnificat. To meet the "other" Mary it is important for the moment to forget the long train of tradition, folklore, patriarchal exegesis, and legend, and whatever else it sweeps along with it. Certainly the "other" Mary has appeared again and again in the history of her glorification, but her real home is in Luke's Gospel. It is possible to tell the story of Mary in many different ways, but let us begin where it really begins, namely, in the succession of biblical women, a tradition that has so often been forgotten and suppressed.

Mary is not alone in this first chapter of Luke's Gospel. There are two women in the story: Mary and Elizabeth. The story begins with the friendship of two women, the solidarity between them, and the way they help one another to bear their "burden." A burden? Yes, for here are two unusual pregnancies: that of Elizabeth, who is already old so that her pregnancy is embarrassing for her, and that of Mary, who is young and unmarried. They have to grapple with this situation. The two women are part of a wider network of women connecting the history of Yahweh with the history of humanity. In the beginning of this story was liberation, the liberation from Egyptian bondage. This liberation is remembered by the Israelites in their creed (Deut. 26:5–19).

The story begins with an act of liberation, a deliverance that was the work of God by human hands. The story of this first liberation itself begins with two courageous women, Shiphrah and Puah, Hebrew midwives who defied Pharaoh's decree that all male Hebrew infants were to be killed at birth and who, by this act of "civil disobedience," saved the lives of the children. The tyrant's command provoked their resistance since their vocation was to bring life into the world and not the reverse.

They honored God, the protector of life, more than they feared Pharaoh. With the help of Pharaoh's daughter, the infant Moses is saved. Here, too, a woman follows her inner voice, her intuition, and refuses to sacrifice the life of a single infant to despotic power. We see emerging the succession of independently minded women that continues with the prophetess Miriam. With Aaron and Moses Miriam led the people into freedom. She sings the oldest liberation song in the Bible:

> Sing to the Lord because he has won a glorious victory. He has thrown the horses and their riders into the sea. (Exod. 15:21)

At the main turning points in the biblical history, therefore, women play an important role: Shiphrah, Puah, and Miriam at the Exodus and Mary and Elizabeth at the beginning of the New Testament. Then at the end of the Gospels Mary Magdalene and other women are at the cross and the empty tomb. This is a succession, a genealogy of a unique kind.

Mary's Vocation

In Luke's account, Mary's story begins with the greeting of an angel. Mary, then, is a woman who listens to angels. "Peace be with you," the angel says to her. Mary is receptive to something magnificent, and God is receptive to her. The act of divine interest and grace contains two promises. First, God will share strength with Mary. Second, the very name Yahweh means God is present and will be there. In other words, it is a promise of strength and an assurance of fidelity. It is given in this one phrase "I stand by your side with all that I have and all that I am, with all my strength" and "you will always be able to count on me!" With such promises in safekeeping, who could fail to be strong? This, then, is the basis of Mary's strength and daring.

At first, however, she is perplexed. She, an unmarried girl, is to become pregnant? The angel helps her to understand the significance of this pregnancy. She is able to see with new eyes that this shameful event of pregnancy out of marriage is a milestone in the history of humanity, the beginning of God's incarnation in humanity. On the basis of this understanding, she answers: "Behold the handmaid of the Lord! Your will be done!"

From that moment on, the interpreters of two thousand years in word, image, and music have abused Mary's response to the angel's announcement. Down to the present day, we have been told that it is an expression of a completely yielding, passive obedience. Is Mary the consenting victim of a predetermined male-divine plan? How many women have been and are being preconditioned for total obedience to men in the churches by an appeal to this example of Mary? How many women have given their consent, in all kinds of relationships and sexual conditions, with the words "may it happen to me as you have said" (Luke 1:38), and in this way justified their submissiveness in their own eyes with a religious trimming.

But such a Mary would not have the right to be mentioned in the same breath as Shiphrah, Puah, and Miriam. Her answer to the angel had a quite different meaning. It is the answer to a prophetic call. It is the same kind of answer as Isaiah's in the hour of his prophetic call. To God's question "Whom shall I send?" he responded with the prayer: "Here am I, send me!" Mary bears the marks of what the Bible puts forward as a significant prophetic calling. God speaks to her through an angel. There is surprise, perplexity, awe, as with all true prophets. Yet she accepts the difficult task of becoming a co-worker, indeed, an agent of the Reign of God. Her answer means: "I am ready to perform this task."

This is not the acceptance of a destiny determined by someone else, but something quite different. Martin Buber, the Jewish theologian, has taught us that the biblical God always gives us the freedom to choose, however urgent may be the divine summons. God calls only those who, however much they may groan at the difficulty, in the deepest sense inwardly approve of this calling. The relation between divine calling and human response is not that between an issued command and a blind obedience. God makes a proposal to which the human being agrees.

Mary stands within the prophetic tradition of the Bible. She responds to God's proposal with a song, an ancient hymn. We call this song the "Magnificat," because the Latin version begins with this word. Mary echoes the song of another woman, the song of Hannah in the Old Testament (1 Sam. 2:1–10). But Mary makes this her own song, selecting the parts that have proved right in her own life. She sings of the utterly reliable strength she has experienced in God.

> My soul exalts God
> and my spirit rejoices in God my savior.
> For God has seen the lowliness of this maiden.
> Behold, from henceforth all generations
> shall call me blessed.
>
> Because God has done mighty things,
> holy is God's name.
> God's mercy endures from generation to generation

for all those who fear God.
God has shown strength with the right hand.
God scatters the proud in the imagination of their hearts.
God dethrones the mighty and uplifts the lowly.
God fills the hungry with good things
and sends the rich empty away.
God remembers the divine mercy
and helps the servant Israel,
as God has spoken to our ancestors
Abraham (and Sarah)
and their children forever.

(Luke 1:46–55)

In her song of thanksgiving Mary introduces one of the great themes of the Reign of God. But she also speaks of her own experience. God blesses and imparts strength to her and God turns an ordinary, insignificant, timid girl into a strong, significant, and courageous woman. God gives her strength to transform the painful and deplorable situation into something strong. With her own body she experiences the transformation of values, effected by the Reign of God. Hence, what is weak is exalted. This is opposite to the value system in the world, where the right of the strong and the economically powerful prevails, whatever the human cost. Mary is made strong, significant.

The Beauty of Mary

Mary is a true prophetess, because she applies her personal experience in a radical way to the real world in which she is living. As a prophetess she will not easily be equalled.

This is as it should be. That is as it will be. God's Reign will overturn the structures of injustice in society. Mercy will not be a small, pious phenomenon, but rather it will take shape in merciful patterns of life. In a continuing exodus, the hungry and the poor are rescued from the merciless conditions in which they live.

This is Mary's vision.

In the Greek text the phrase "God's Reign" implies that something that has been stated in the past continues into the future. This is not done once for all or only in the future. God has given another value system to people. From now on this value system remains the driving force for God's people. These new values are expressed in the prophetic work of Mary and determined people like her in today's world. God's presence in history becomes visible and effective in the work of the children of God.

But the challenge comes only now. To create human relationships worthy of God and pleasing to God, it is necessary to set right the scales of divine justice, which have been distorted by human injustice. The mighty must step down, indeed are cast down, if they don't step down voluntarily. This is neither the revenge of the marginalized nor a divine punishment. What Mary sees, rather, is the inherent dynamic of God's Reign. Those who stand in the way of God's just orders must resign, so that the balance can be restored. This is not a natural spectacle but something achieved by God using the hands of God's people. The poor, however, do not ascend and occupy the vacated throne of the powerful in order to continue to play just a new version of the old game. No one will sit on the throne except the glorious justice of God.

The joy of Zacchaeus, the tax collector who voluntarily returned his unjust gain after he had gained back his human heart through the encounter with Jesus, awaits the rich who are sent empty away. He had silenced his heart himself for profit reasons. Zacchaeus no longer wants to be a hindrance to God's Reign. He expresses his conversion by giving back his ill-gotten gains. Jesus tells him: "Today, salvation, liberation, has come to this house." This converting power that restores the scales of divine justice can be experienced by the "weak" Marys and the "rich" Zacchaeuses in this world, both of whom dwell within all of us, women and men alike. God's power does not abandon anyone from conversion, the poor or the rich. And so she sings

> God remembers mercy
> and helps the servant Israel,
> as God has spoken to our ancestors
> Abraham (and Sarah)
> and their children for ever!

So Mary is uplifted to an incomparable prophetic greatness. Fearlessly and unambiguously she points to the revolutions of the Reign of God in this world. There is no "two kingdoms doctrine" spoiling this connection. Such radical sentences do not come easily to our lips. Mary's vision is a bold one, and it is not easy to decide whether it is Mary who is speaking to her unborn child, or her child who is already speaking to us through her. Mary has started out on the prophetic messianic road with the child within her womb. But it is not enough to have vision; another quality is required, which comes out as we look at this text from women's perspective.

We would not be doing justice to this text if we failed to see it specifically through the lens of our history as women. Mary's prophetic message also concerns the structures of power between women and men. Within these structures most women today are still among the powerless and the poor. The technical term for this is "the feminization of poverty." We have come to know in greater detail the extent to which the patriarchal society of the ancient world assigned a subordinate place to women. It was a world in which religious knowledge was communicated through men, the priests. It was unheard of for an insignificant and inexperienced girl to have direct experience of God. Mary dared to communicate divine insights — and what great insights! — and dared to persist in doing so. We women today who do this from a new perspective should take this to heart. The only qualification she had for doing so was a promise, a vision, the word of an angel, the word of this outer/inner voice leading her. Mary, whose word as a woman carried no weight in the public life of her day, anticipated the reversal of sexist power structures. Had she been obedient to the patriarchal values of her time, she would never have opened her mouth at all and never become God's co-worker. But by speaking up in this way, she challenged the male power structure in religion. Mary already lived in a new order of values in which she had an intrinsic worth and made her own decisions.

The beauty of Mary, her authenticity, lies not in her humble submission but in the inner harmony that unites her with the divine will. She does not obey an alien will, but acts on the basis of her deepest insight that this "plan" to send a savior to humanity, the Messiah, springs from a clear-sighted love and must therefore be "of God." This seeing "obedience" of Mary has assumed a quite different quality and therefore requires a new word to express it. It constrains Mary, and us after her, to disobey the patriarchal scheme of things where it inhibits life. It constrains her, and us, to step out of conformity and to contradict a famished, racist, weapon-crazy, misogynous, and polluted world, by radical affirmations, affirming life, a life to be restored. Any woman or man who acts as Mary's song recommends chooses to be bound to God with a greater loyalty than to the patriarchal values that have long been rejected even by many men. Therefore, "beauty" and "revolt" are not mutually exclusive. Mary's strength to resist the false orders of the world in which she lives is derived from her inner harmony with the divine will. A new Mary stands before us, a Mary who is beautiful because she dares to speak up for the better life that is God's will. She is "born again," she is a new woman who has experienced a radical conversion, namely, from submissiveness to active assent and to independent action. From silence to speech. For herself and for us all, she achieved this new identity. It is to be hoped that never again will we let ourselves be robbed of it. The new vision goes together and goes only with a new identity. New/old visions mean new/old commitments. This is what the Magnificat tells us.

Using Power

The Power to Communicate

Christa Berger

I believe that one day it will be discovered that women are human beings. Yes, in many senses equal to us. I believe that one day they themselves will discover that. And . . . then. . . . Well, I think that then they will rise and ask to be considered part of the human race and that, as a consequence, there will be difficulties.

— Mark Twain

Women have discovered that they are part of the human race and that they, like men, are created in the image of God. The consequences of this discovery, as predicted by Mark Twain, cause difficulties for both sexes.

We live in a post–feminist movement era, and so we have many examples of how women were excluded from making history and made it nevertheless. I want to begin by giving two examples that show how the way facts were interpreted excluded the significance of the presence of women. Psychoanalysis and Christianity would have been very different if women had been taken into account in these instances alone.

The first example is of a myth, recounted by Freud in *Civilization and Its Discontents*, explaining how primitive men conquered fire. Freud's theory suggests that fire already existed before man, through spontaneous combustion. When the primitive man found that strange manifestation of energy coming from nature to be in his way, he used to practice a sort of game or ritual that consisted of extinguishing the fire with the stream of his urine. It was a kind of enacted sexual relation in which the man, with his potency, dominated and pacified the magic and unknown force that nature placed in his way. Only when the first man declined this sexual pleasure and, instead of extinguishing fire, preserved it and brought it home to his cave, did he learn its secrets and profited from it.

When Freud interpreted this myth, the possibility that this first man, who declined to test his potency against the fire, could have been a woman never occurred to him. His whole theory of male and female sexuality would have another perspective if this possibility had at least come up as a hypothesis. This is not to mention the significance that women would have gained as "discoverers" of the benefits of the fire.

The other example I want to refer to is well known to all of us. It is the story of the resurrection, which is considered to be one of the foundation texts of Christianity. This text, however, needed a "feminist theology" to receive a treatment in which the importance of Mary Magdalene, who saw the resurrected Lord, was recognized.

The presence of women is part of the description of the resurrection, but their presence has not been seen as relevant or an issue that calls for reflection. If Christianity had recognized that the Lord had *chosen* to appear to women and that they were the ones asked to proclaim the good news, certainly women would have been given another role in the institutional church.

I believe that the process of communication is made up of the production, interpretation, and distribution of ideas. The production and interpretation of ideas have always been masculine. The distribution of ideas, even though carried out by women (for instance in school), also carries the masculine imprint, since women have deeply internalized the current worldview.

The Bible was written and interpreted by men. The ideas contained in it belonged to men. The traditional way of reading the Bible characterizes God as masculine, and we say without questioning: "God the almighty Father, Our Father who is in heaven." We forget that God said: "I am who I am" (Exod. 3:14). God does not identify Godself with anything or anybody. This identification of God with the masculine led to androcentric and discriminatory behavior. If God is father, the father is the one who was made in the image and resemblance of God and is therefore more valuable. The mother/woman was made from Adam's rib and as such is an appendix.

For a long time the Bible presented the dominant worldview and was thus the source for behavioral norms. It is no longer the only source. Another source for behavioral norms now is mass media.

Here I want to present some reflections regarding the role of women in contemporary dominant forms of communication.

The Power of Television

Each historical moment has a dominant form of communication. There may be several, but they are always overshadowed by the main one. In my country, Brazil, the dominant medium is television. It is the most sophisticated form of communication in its combination of verbal and nonverbal communication. It is truly a *mass* medium capable of bringing image and sound into our homes. This entails a huge financial investment, hours of work by many researchers in different parts of the world, and astounding technological developments. These huge financial investments make the process irreversible. To think about the relation between media and women is to think about the economic and social function that the medium has in relation to the whole of society, and the impact it has on women. Television has the role of legitimizing, giving credit to, and making socially acceptable those values that a capitalist society needs to maintain itself.

For some, television is a showcase of the consumer society and a factory of ready-made identities for people. In Brazil, television does not only present reality, but it makes it, building a reality that is convenient to the dominant class. In the case of women, the media portray an image that serves the interests not only of the dominant class, but also of the transnational structures of power. The worst thing about this is that this image, this identity, becomes the only possible way of being woman — an ideal woman, ideal for the masculine patterns, for the power structures and the consumer society. It is far from the real woman that we recognize in our aspirations and desires when we are able to think for ourselves.

I live in a country in which the majority of the population does not have access to food, housing, transportation, employment, land, health, leisure, or pleasure. This generates a situation of minimum subsistence in which misery, violence, high infant mortality, and social and sexual discrimination predominate. However, in this same country there is a television network considered one of the best in the world, which reaches 90 million out of the 130 million of Brazil's inhabitants. This network promotes the idea of the ideal woman. She is beautiful and well dressed. She works to feel independent. She is happy because she has access to consumer goods. She is a good mother because she buys advertised products for her children.

This ideal model of women received in our homes, through soap operas, commercials, or news broadcasts, is a representation that coincides with very few women's practical reality. But television is not concerned with the women who do not have buying power. After all, television is commercial and is directed to those who have the power to buy.

To the other women who receive these same values, ideas, and information, the only thing left is frustration and guilt. The question of social inequality is identified as an individual question, of individual performance and competence. The implications are false and cruel. It is a cruelty to promulgate a set of values based exclusively on buying power in a society in which not even 20 percent of the population can effectively achieve these values. The double message running through our poor countries can explain much of the violence and frustration in which we live. Double messages generate neurosis. A Brazilian psychoanalyst, Maria Rita Kehl, goes further and says that today we already are a schizophrenic nation. We receive messages saying travel, buy, save, have life insurance, take care of the future, even though we are a population that does not have the means to take care of the present, to educate our children, or to survive.

It is in this environment of cruelty that we also find the appropriation of women's bodies. The female body has value only if it is thin, if it smells good, and if it is covered with jewels and furs.

The worship of the body characterizes the loneliness of the modern world. The body that appears on television is all image. Woman is body, but a body fragmented into breasts, legs, and bottom. It is a body that sells and can be sold. Historically, woman is the apple. She is the factor of temptation, and the commercials know how to play up this aspect of seduction. Historically, also, women have a price, through the dowry they bring to their husbands, through the body that serves for prostitution, through the fragments of the body that sell merchandise. When the purchased merchandise is identified with the body that sold it, the woman is assigned a price once more. The price is proportionate to her power of seduction.

The women I see portrayed on my country's television are feminine because they are submissive; pretty because they are white, thin, and rich; happy because they consume; in the workplace because it is modern; and interested in politics to be interesting to male eyes. It only confirms the premise that women exist for the satisfaction of the other.

To learn how to satisfy the other is the main purpose of our learning. It justifies the existence of so many feminine magazines, giving out tips and advice all with the same purpose: how to win *that* man. In other words, what we learn are strategies of manipulation that not only prevent true relationships, but also alienate us from ourselves. Passivity, submission, and nothingness are products manufactured like merchandise to be consumed by men and women. Like all consumer goods, they too have a price, a very high price. It is our own lives that are at risk, since we get lost from ourselves. We lose the possibility of love. Love can no longer happen between equals. A whole set of conditional behaviors, such as servitude and submission, makes us men and women almost incompatible with love.

The media in Brazil do not portray the peasant or factory-working women, or the women torn between career and motherhood. Television does not create values in a vacuum. It does not arbitrarily build stereotypes, but it starts with the fantasies of those who watch it. For women to remain glued to the television, there have to be elements that enter into our fantasies and fascinate us. The pertinent question is: what is so fascinating? To put it another way: what makes women of such different economic, cultural, and emotional backgrounds follow the plot of a soap opera every day and get emotional to the point of tears?

The ability of television to communicate through image and to reach people in the intimacy of their homes makes it possible to present messages that are highly emotional and act as censors, suggesting what women ought to believe. In so doing television facilitates the psychological process of projection and identification. It is in this space that models, stars, and mythological beings are created, and they, in turn, become paradigms of behavior.

What paralyzes us in front of the screen in this process of identification is that television deals with our myths, our most archaic experiences, through which we unconsciously cleanse ourselves. This process of living through the screen the myth of seduction and castration, the primary scene spoken of by Freud, makes the television today the great psychiatric couch. But instead of giving us emancipation, it makes us relapse. Indeed, the whole idea that television takes away stress, that it relaxes, that it provides positive role models, occurs insofar as modern people symbolically relates to their fears and afflictions through television in the same way primitive people did through magic and ritual practices.

The way we relate to the media is a type of ritual. We watch the same programs, at the same time, sitting in the same chair. There is repetition in the act of reading the newspaper or following certain radio or television programs. So we are ready and available to receive whatever will come. One author relates the Brazilian soap operas at the end of the day to the habit of going to church. The end of the day is a time of gathering, sometimes with fear of the night or the next day. Sometimes it is filled with affliction. The soap operas, then, may substitute for the rite of going to church, but the psychological need to listen and search for words of comfort remains. This is why the plot of these soap operas is always extremely funny or romantic and always filled with great suffering.

Women's Alternatives

The question of mass communication and women is related to two issues: the representation of women — the way in which women are portrayed in the media — and the moment of reception — how these images are appropriated and "copied" collectively by women.

Certainly it is not easy to respond fully to these issues. It is encouraging to know that much work in different parts of the world has been done to understand this problem. We already have a critical inventory of mass media production. Even more encouraging, however, is knowing that in other parts of the world people are criticizing mass communication and offering alternative proposals.

What are the alternatives?

In Latin America we have a series of communication centers concerned with producing alternative messages regarding women. The Unity of Women's Alternative Communication of the Latin Institute of Transnational Studies (ILET) has organized seminars and studied data in relation to women's issues. They have found examples of women's theater, videos, slides, magazines, and radio programs that talk about different group experiences. They have also found some soap operas that deal with women's reality from a new, more humane point of view. Women's alternative communication in Latin America is closely related to alternative communication in general, that is, it has the perspective of the emancipation of the people as a whole, and women in particular.

The international network of women has a very important center in Latin America, ISIS International, located in Chile. Since 1984, it has published magazines along with other Third World groups and made available special supplements with news on women's networks, addresses, lists of publications, and notices of meetings and conferences. In Brazil there is also a women's network that puts out a monthly bulletin called *Cunhari,* an Indian name meaning river of women. It also makes available to women's groups different types of information, and it facilitates the exchange of videos used in awareness raising. Many of these works come from a Christian perspective, point out new directions, and criticize the treatment of women in the consumer society and mass communication. Also, many centers for alternative communication have been created with the support of churches.

There is also a relation between the opening of the churches for women's ordained ministry and the churches' branching into new ministries, such as ministries with the poor. In the same way as the oppressed are the ones better equipped to reflect on oppression, so are women, with the history of discrimination, capable of proposing a re-reading of the Bible. This is already happening. We are the ones who can rediscover the biblical revelation. This is alternative communication. The message is the same, but it is read with new eyes. To allow women's eyes to read the word of God is the great challenge. This word belongs to everyone and cannot, therefore, be the monopoly of any type of power, whether economic or masculine.

Traditions die when new generations are not capable of recovering fundamental questions and giving new meaning to them. This is what happens with theological reflection. For a tradition to remain alive, it needs to be constantly reinterpreted, and this is what women can do, with their experience of absence and oppression. Women must add emancipatory actions to the theoretical reflection.

To Be a Servant Leader

Lynda Katsuno-Ishii

There was a woman who had suffered terribly from severe bleeding for twelve years, even though she had been treated by many doctors. She had spent all her money, but instead of getting better she got worse all the time. She had heard about Jesus, so she came in the crowd behind him, saying to herself, "If I just touch his clothes I will get well." She touched his cloak, and her bleeding stopped at once; and she had the feeling inside herself that she was healed of her trouble. At once Jesus knew that power had gone out of him, so he turned round in the crowd and asked, "Who touched my clothes?" His disciples answered, "You see how the people are crowding you; why do you ask who touched you?" But Jesus kept looking round to see who had done it. The woman realized what had happened to her, so she came, trembling with fear, knelt at his feet, and told him the whole truth. Jesus said to her, "My daughter, your faith has made you well. Go in peace and be healed of your trouble." (Mark 5:25–34 TEV)

One almost hesitates to use this story, as it is often used in so many other contexts, but I very much like Carter Heyward's exegesis: that the woman who touched Jesus' garments felt in her body that she was healed of her disease; Jesus, perceiving in himself that power had gone out from him, turned about in the crowd. There is a flow of power, a reciprocal situation in which both persons are affected by what is happening between them: Jesus is vulnerable to touch, relation, the healing process, not as the one who heals but as the one who participates in the healing. Jesus tells the woman to go in peace, her faith has made her well. Jesus does not say that he or God has healed the women, but acknowledges that the woman has played a vital role in what has happened to her, that she has participated and shared in the process of her healing.

The power that goes forth from Jesus, the power released by the woman's reaching and touching in faith, is a power quite unlike the principalities and powers within, between and among us, that seek control and domination over our own lives and the lives of others. The power that goes forth from Jesus has nothing to do with wealth, status, orthodoxy or conformity to established patterns of thought or behavior or feeling in society. The power that goes forth from Jesus is *dynamism* — raw, spontaneous, unmediated power — which breaks down established roles of control and possession and sets the stage for a new experience of power as reciprocal; a power that is shared in faith and trust, moving, given, received, passed on, celebrated.[1]

I use this lengthy citation as the basis for a brief reflection. There are many aspects and dimensions to the word "power," all of which provoke much interest and reflection, but it would be impossible to go into an in-depth study here. Instead, I offer some thoughts and reflections on the concept of power as described in this citation from Carter Heyward, especially as it relates to women.

The Challenge of Power

My first instinct is to think on a structural level, because in the world, in our cultures, in our societies, and in our churches, women have been in the position of being dominated. Often considered the weak and the powerless, women have also become the medium of God's rescuing power. Women all over the world, at whatever point in their journey of liberation, are beginning to react and respond. There are many unjust power structures in and outside the church that often enable a few to dominate the many, and often the *few* are men and the *many* are women. Nations, groups, systems, structures often hold the power to decide other people's lives, but when they love and hold onto power in such a way that it denies God's gift of justice, unity, sharing, and responsibility, then it becomes destructive and unjust. God's way is to share power as Jesus did in Mark 5, to share it among ourselves, to empower each other.

This calls on us all to locate and study power in our own contexts and our own situation. The kind of community we are searching for is possible only when women and men struggle against those systems and unjust structures that oppress women. Such a struggle will one day empower women to burst out of their tombs of oppression. In this sense, power is always in the context of justice.

I occasionally wonder, however, if some women find it difficult to understand what happened in the story of Mark 5. This is not an easy thing to acknowledge and write. I have had the opportunity to attend many international, ecumenical women's conferences, and on some occasions, I have sat silently, deep in thought, watching many of the women in positions of "authority" fall into the traditional power traps into which our male counterparts are often accused of falling. I ask myself why, and why do women also use power in a negative way that puts down and manipulates other women? Why do some women in authority/power lack a certain element of humanness? Why do they forget the gifts that make them creative and strong, in spite of structures and systems that have marginalized and disempowered them?

In a church world dominated by men, must women take on qualities similar to those that have often been considered negative in order to recognize and claim the power. Is it because women are so accustomed to thinking of themselves as powerless? Is it because for centuries women have seen themselves as the model of servanthood in the church? Has this service — doing things for other people — led them to believe that this is to give up power? As women break down walls of traditional power, how do they begin to reconcile the idea that servanthood and service mean the same thing for men and women? Are women afraid to share power because they have seen how men have "given up" power (which is not the same as the power that went forth from Jesus in Mark 5) only to engineer things so that they somehow get the power back?

These are just a few of the questions that I asked myself as I sat deep in thought through those sessions. In trying to answer these questions, I realized that the people who received the power most responsibly are those who receive it in humbleness and humility, those who will always act for the good of the community. Women who, once given power, must always prove capable and "worthy" of this responsibility must understand that they should not seek anything for themselves, but in roles of moderators, executive staff, coordinators, etc., must seek to be servant leaders. This is the challenge. The essential for all people with power is that they are servants before they are leaders or bosses. People who assume responsibility to prove something tend to be dominating and controlling because they need to see themselves at the top. Or perhaps they are looking for prestige, in which case they will often exercise their power and responsibility badly; it is always sad when women fall into this kind of situation. The irony, given women's lives of servanthood in the church throughout all these centuries, is that as they receive power and some measure of authority and responsibility, they must first seek to be servants.

Soft Whispers

The theme for the World Council of Churches' Seventh Assembly in Australia in 1991 was "Come Holy Spirit — Renew the Whole Creation." As we often use the term "power of the Holy Spirit," I shall make a link between the assembly theme and power. So often, we think of power in what is strong, what is mighty, like the "powerful wind blowing at Pentecost." But one Bible study enabler helped people to recognize the power of the gentle breeze, as God reveals God to Elijah in 1 Kings 19.[2] In this story, it is important to remember the circumstances in which God appears to Elijah — in a cave that is dark, silent, in a mountain. Elijah is alone, but has the wisdom of heart to be able to recognize God in the gentle breeze (the Jerusalem Bible uses this term; Today's English Version uses the term "soft whisper") and in these very extraordinary and unexpected circumstances.

How often does society, do women themselves, fail to recognize God's gifts and the power given to them through people in their midst? Women, people with disabilities, children waft through people's lives like a gentle breeze, but as the "soft whispers," they are considered weak and powerless. Often this is because of stigmas, structures, and systems in society and cultures that continue to marginalize, to disempower. How can women use the gifts they have, as women, to empower each other? How can they learn to see each other's gifts as strengths that can be shared, going forth one to another? How can women come to see their gifts in a new light, not as signs of weakness but as signs of strength, so that women can develop new models of leadership in community that do not fall into traditional male-oriented traps? How can women develop within themselves that inner wisdom as experienced by Elijah?

I have always believed in community. I believe we come together in so much of our work as community. But community does not come easily. As more structures are broken down and more paths open for women in the church and society, we must find a way of receiving and sharing power, so that in strength and humbleness we can build community as servant leaders.

Notes

1. Carter Heyward, *Our Passion for Justice — Images of Power, Sexuality, and Liberation* (New York: Pilgrim Press, 1984), 118.
2. Bible studies led by Dr. Maria Teresa Procile Santiso at the World Council of Churches consultation, held in Bangkok, Thailand, in March 1989.

Bibliography

Gill, David, ed. *Gathered for Life*. Geneva: WCC Publications, 1984.
Heyward, Carter. *Our Passion for Justice: Images of Power, Sexuality and Liberation*. New York: Pilgrim Press, 1984.
The Mud Flower Collective. *God's Fierce Whimsy*. Ed. Carter Heyward. New York: Pilgrim Press, 1985.
Vanier, Jean. *Community and Church*. London: Darton, Longman and Todd, 1979.
Weber, Hans Ruedi. *Power: Focus for a Biblical Theology*. Geneva: WCC Publications, 1990.
Wilson, Frederick R., ed. *The San Antonio Report*. Geneva: WCC Publications, 1990.

Practical Power

Wendy S. Robins

Within the two and a half years in which this book has had its genesis my struggle to come to a positive model to suggest for women's use of power has been ongoing. My head whirls with stories, stories of women's struggles, from this book, from other books, from my own life, and the life of my friends. Many of them form partially written parts of what I want to say — some written in my head, others on paper, all tailing off and without conclusion, because my stories are always negative and lacking the positive endings with which I seek to redress the balance.

Maybe what I realize now is that the end of our searching is not yet. As women who still face oppression of various kinds it seems that, as yet, the strong have failed to learn to care for the weak. Perhaps our power will finally come from naming the fact that here and now we remain flawed and searching for solutions.

Gaining Power

Over many years now women have struggled to be recognized within existing societal power bases. Recognizing and analyzing patriarchal structures and systems has led to women, singularly and as groups, working to gain a position within these structures, challenging them and seeking to assert their right to a part in the decision-making process in their lives, families, work, churches, and societies. In fact, wherever groups of people gather, women are seeking to become fully equal in all that occurs.

As the final decade of the twentieth century progresses, the successes of these strategies can be seen. There are still comparatively few women in positions of power in business, church, and society, yet there are more than there were thirty years ago, and so our struggle has not been in vain.

Women's struggles, however, are not at an end, and it seems responsible to consider what our next moves might be. My confusion in this regard lies in the stories and events that I have heard, and participated in, that leave me to question whether women are simply trying to oust men from powerful positions merely to insert themselves in the same roles, with the same powers, and, most importantly, with the same disregard for others for which we have constantly chided our male counterparts.

Stories to Explain

Picture two women's conferences, large international gatherings designed to empower women in their daily lives and in their lives within the church.

Picture too the power structures within these. Some of the women are used to participating in international gatherings; they feel sure of their ground, clear about their purposes. They are aware of the significance of certain political and social nuances; they are, in short, the leaders of the pack.

Other women are attending such a conference for the first time. Their ability to speak the given conference language is more limited; they feel impoverished and marginalized by their powerful sisters *who must, surely, know best.*

The power in such situations often lies with women from the North, the economically well-developed countries, who are "richer" than their sisters. Yet this is not always the case. Sometimes power lies within those who represent women who are especially oppressed, not simply because of their gender but because of their color and place of birth. They come to prominence as women who can speak for themselves and others, and thus they gain power. The acquisition of power itself is not negative, but sometimes the way we use it is.

Once having gained power women have responsibility to use it wisely and for the good of the majority. Yet too often, as at the two conferences envisaged, power is used to preserve power for those who have it. Having fought hard for positions, women retain them and use their power in much the same way as men — pushing their own points of view, in the sure belief that they are right, and ignoring others. These situations cause many women a great deal of anger, frustration, and pain, because they find themselves feeling as if they have entered into the same oppressive systems that they were fighting.

Women often suggest that they use power nonhierarchically. But what evidence is there to support these assertions?

The Conferences

It is very hot and the conference is drawing to a close. Plenaries are getting longer and more difficult and the number of papers to be corrected and revised after each is increasing.

Lunch time arrives and the administrative staff go off to work on the documentation. The conference delegates go to eat lunch. Imagine then the feelings aroused when lunchtime ends and no one has thought to inquire of the administrative staff whether they would like to be brought some food. Why is it that the women at the conference succeeded in making these staff invisible, expecting them to produce the papers as required but not to need feeding or consideration?

Consider too this situation. The executive staff person and one of her administrative staff are travelling together on business. They attend a meeting at which they are both introduced by a third woman, someone who knows them both well and their contribution to the overall work. How must the administrative person feel to be introduced more or less as the odd-job girl with little importance in the department? How does the executive staff person feel? How can she react in this most difficult of circumstances?

My sadness lies in the apparent fact that once women have gained power they somehow forget to look after their sisters who have less power. People are treated with less respect than they deserve. Administrative staff are, on occasions, expected to do the impossible and not thanked for achieving it — a situation about which women would complain bitterly if it were men who had the expectations. Women are hurt by other women as they struggle to assert their rights and to be powerful.

The compassion and kindness that is shown during the struggle get mislaid as the struggle ends for those who gain power, and life becomes as intolerable under their leadership as it was under men's. Indeed it may seem more intolerable, because these are our own sisters with whom we are fighting.

I remember too wanting to scream at the way women treat other women who are different from them. At one conference the women of color were not in a minority, but in a particular grouping there was only one black woman in a group of white women. She suffered for it. For all her skills and experience she was made to feel powerless and useless. She was perceived as having less experience simply because the white women considered their culture to be superior. Such examples are not concerned only with the interaction of black and white, but also with language, race, level of education, and different abilities.

The Organization

Or picture the scene in a large organization. This organization has a policy of employing at least 50 percent women and a good percentage of young people, people from ethnic minorities, or people with disabilities. Part of that organization realizes that it does not meet these criteria especially in regard to the employment of women in "senior" positions. When appointments are to be made it is agreed that everything possible shall be done to ensure the appointment of women, at least until the target of equal representation is reached.

An appointment is to be made. Women are sought, but not quite in the highways and byways. There is a view, which holds some truth, that more might have been done. The person wishing to appoint waits some months for a promising woman who, finally, withdraws.

A man is found who has all the experience and qualities necessary to do the job. Indeed he is ideal. Save for his gender.

A staff meeting is called at which it is explained that this appointment is to be made. Staff members point out that prior to this another staff appointment was made, by the same people, also of a male. The main objectors are female; the person perceived as the prime mover in both appointments is also a woman.

To this point it is possible to see "right" on both sides, although I guess that most women would wish other women to stand firmly with them. But believing that all that could be done had been done seems enough. Then events begin to take another turn.

From this point on organizing begins, which in many senses ostracizes and isolates the woman making the appointments. She is seen to be identifying with the male senior management, as memos begin to fly and maneuvers to take place. The person needing to make the appointments ends up feeling battered and hurt, saying that her female colleagues are treating her less considerately than her male colleagues. Unable to understand the vehemence of the feelings she has aroused against herself, she begins to wonder what feminism is really about. Never one to have been identified as a radical, or even a very forthright feminist, she now wonders what the point was if women could not understand each other's points of view.

Interestingly, her isolation was perceived by other women in the department and gradually they rallied to support her. They too had begun to feel undermined by the strength of advocacy and lack of compromise of their other colleague. The situation continues, a form of peace has evolved, but the pain and sense of injustice on both sides will take a long time to heal.

Considering the stories and positions of women featured in this book and the implicit statements made on women's advocacy, I have been led to consider what is an appropriate mode of leadership. In what ways can women ensure that all are valued and have a voice? Recently, when reading the New Testament lesson in the Eucharist at a conference, I was struck by these words:

> Don't do anything from selfish ambition or from a cheap desire to boast, but be humble towards one another, always considering others better than yourselves. And look out for one another's interests, not just for your own. (Phil. 2:3–4 TEV)

What leapt off the page at me was the final phase. We are so used to being told to look out for other's and that others are more important than we are that it came as a shock to me to be told, not only to look out for other's interests, but for my own too. I wondered if this was the key. Sometimes I think we spend so much time holding on to the power we have gained because we have little or no belief in an ability to share power. It is mine or it is yours, not it is ours. And I wonder if this is partly the result of being told to look out for other people's interests and thus implicitly feeling that we must ignore our own. Recognizing that our own interests are important and valid might help us, as we take positions of power, to focus too on other people's needs and wants.

Being clear about who we are as individuals may help us to become clearer about our own needs and how to try to serve the needs of others.

An open and consultative style of leadership is energy- and time-consuming. Listening to other people's ideas and thoughts, sifting everything and then trying to reach consensus, inevitably takes much longer than sitting down, trying to imagine the various viewpoints, and deciding alone.

At times working collectively seems too hard, and even within this model there will always be the stronger women who group together. Yet sticking with consultation and consensus through all its difficulties can mean that people feel affirmed. They grow in confidence and a willingness to participate if they feel that they are valued and that their ideas are worthwhile.

This does not, however, mean that it is never appropriate for an individual to be responsible for the final decision making. Often it is necessary for organizations or groups to have one designated chair, president, director, or coordinator. This role can be a difficult one because there are times when to balance the interests of different people and groups seems impossible. Even harder are the times when the unpopular decision is necessary, the one that the "leader" believes to be right even if it is the minority view. At such times decisions must be made and the responsible person must do what she believes to be right. Here openness and honesty are important, because if groups are seen to work collectively then when a decision is made others will respect it as a considered opinion.

But the key is to listen, to weigh all sides, to consider our own interests and the interests of others, to recognize when we are the right people for a job and when we are not, to give praise to others when it is due, to be encouraging, and to be willing to admit to failure and mistakes.

To develop a practical style of leadership in this model takes a great deal of time and is often painful, but it is only in this way that women will find new, more acceptable styles of leadership and not simply replace old male models with new, equally oppressive female ones.

About the Authors

Christa Berger is a Brazilian journalist who teaches communication at the University of Río Grande do Sul. She lives in Porto Alegre and is involved in the Brazilian Ecumenical Group on Christian Communication.

Violet Cucciniello Little comes from the United States of America. She is a graduate of the Lutheran Theological Seminary in Philadelphia and is ordained in the Lutheran Church. One of her major concerns is writing and preparing material from women's perspectives.

Wanda Deifelt is Brazilian. When she wrote the chapter that appears in this book, she was doing doctoral work in feminist theology and Lutheran theology at Garrett Evangelical Theological Seminary/ Northwestern University in Evanston, Illinois, U.S.A. She has now completed these studies and is teaching at the Escola Superior de Teología in São Leopoldo, Brazil.

Musimbi Kanyoro is the Executive Secretary for Women in Church and Society with the Lutheran World Federation in Geneva. From Kenya, Musimbi is a linguistic and biblist by profession. In addition to teaching at Nairobi University, Musimbi worked for many years as a translation consultant with the United Bible Societies.

Lynda Katsuno-Ishii is from Canada. When she wrote the chapter that appears in this book, she lived and worked in Geneva where she was a consultant to the Programme Unit on Education and Renewal of the World Council of Churches, being its special advisor on issues of disability. Lynda acts as a worship facilitator at many conferences and gatherings. She has now returned to Canada.

Constance F. Parvey was the coordinator of the Community of Women and Men study of the World Council of Churches for four years. From the United States of America, she is a Lutheran pastor in Massachusetts.

Ranjini Rebera was born in Sri Lanka. Specializing in communication, she has lived and worked throughout South East Asia. She lives now in Australia. Ranjini has facilitated workshops throughout the world on women and power.

Wendy S. Robins is from England. For the last fourteen years she has worked as an adult educator in the churches and is currently working as Education Secretary for the United Society for the Propagation of the Gospel, an Anglican mission agency. She is training for the Anglican ministry.

Raquel Rodríguez is from Puerto Rico. Recently ordained as a Lutheran pastor, she lives in Costa Rica where she works as a researcher in the Department of Ecumenical Research. She focuses on women's struggles and publishes materials from a Latin American ideological perspective.

Jean Sindab is from the United States of America. When she wrote this chapter she was an executive secretary with the Program to Combat Racism of the World Council of Churches, Geneva. She presently works for the National Council of Churches in the USA, in New York.

Bärbel von Wartenberg-Potter is from Germany. Formerly the director for the Sub-Unit of Women in Church and Society of the World Council of Churches, Geneva, she was living and working in Jamaica when she wrote the chapter that appears here. She is now a Lutheran pastor in Germany.